Collective Dating

A Collection of 12 One-Act Plays

by

VB Leghorn

SAMUEL FRENCH

FOUNDED 1830

NEW YORK HOLLYWOOD LONDON TORONTO

SAMUELFRENCH.COM

IMPORTANT BILLING AND CREDIT REQUIREMENTS

All producers of COLLECTIVE DATING *must* give credit to the Author of the Play in all programs distributed in connection with performances of the Play, and in all instances in which the title of the Play appears for the purposes of advertising, publicizing or otherwise exploiting the Play and/or a production. The name of the Author *must* appear on a separate line on which no other name appears, immediately following the title and *must* appear in size of type not less than fifty percent of the size of the title type.

DATES & NUTS, Five One-Acts About Dating In Modern Times, from *Collective Dating*, premièred at The Foothill Theatre Conservatory in Los Altos Hills, California on April 13, 2007. The Production Director was Janis Bergmann, Stage Managers were Suzie Poulson and Arturo Dirzo, with lighting design by Bruce McLeod, costumes by Ashley Rogers, Brennan Holness and Ryan Rusca, each with the following directors and casts:

SPEED DATING

Director	Suzie Poulson
WOMAN A	Sara Krindel
MAN B	Matt Miyake
WOMAN C	Sarah Young
MAN F	Daniel Mitchell
WOMAN E	Olga Adelung
MAN D	Timothy Goble
MATRON	Jake Van Tuyl

THE DRAG OF DATING

Director	Lauren Mack
AARON	Arturo Dirzo
SCOTT	Alex Hero
JIMMY	Derrick Brooks
CONNER	Jake Van Tuyl
STAGE MANAGER	Sarah Young

THE DATING GAME

Director	Brennan Holness
LUCY	Marvina Reasons
CHUCK	James Appleby II
BACHELOR NO. 1	Sam Acheson
BACHELOR NO. 2	Jerome Sephers
BACHELOR NO. 3	Michael Vitols
ANNOUNCER	Timothy Goble

INTERNET DATING

Director	Ashley Rogers
JEFF	Joey Paris
GEORGE	Ryan Rusca
STEVE	Takuya Tsuchiya
JANIE	Mari Muraoka
JULIE	Juliana Schoedinger
HARRISON	Patrick Borella

CREATIVE DATING

Director . . . . Kimberly Johnson
CRYSTAL . . . . Aurora Simcovich
MEGAN . . . . Shannon Tierney
JORDAN . . . . Drew Moore
POLICEMAN . . . . Matt Miyake
MAN . . . . Daniel Mitchell
WOMAN . . . . Olga Adelung

PRE-DATING premièred as part of Ross Valley Players' Alternative Works in Progress series on November 18, 2007 in Ross, California. The production was directed by Mark Shepard with the following cast:

NALA . . . . Debbie Warren
NOLO . . . . Pat Barr
ARG . . . . Irving Schulman
CREBO . . . . Mark Shepard

TABLE OF CONTENTS

1. Creative Dating

Two desperate women rob a bank – not rob, just delay business for a while – in an effort to get a date with the man of their dreams. 3 men,
3 WOMEN
JORDAN
POLICEMAN
MAN OF FLOOR
MEGAN
CRYSTAL
WOMAN ON FLOOR

2. Blind Dating

Two blind lawyers meet on a blind date at a golf course where they find mistrust, deceit and a possible soul mate. 2 men, 2 women
JOE
TED
LAUREN
ASHLEY

3. Internet Dating

The Love Guru helps lost souls find love through an Internet dating seminar that teaches more then just how to hook up. 4 men, 2 women
JEFF
GEORGE
STEVE
HARRISON
JANIE
JULIE

4. Speed Dating

The clock ticks down on three couples thrown together in a round of speed dating. 3 men, 3 women, 1 swing
MAN B
MAN D
MAN F
WOMAN A
WOMAN C
WOMAN E
GUARD

5.   The Drag of Dating
Four female impersonators help a friend break off a bad relationship with a psychotic girlfriend who happens to be their stage manager. 4 men

CONNER
AARON
SCOTT
JIMMY

6.   The Dating Game
Three bachelors, one bachelorette and a delusional proprietor of a wacky dating service try to find truth and love through an afternoon mock-up of the Dating Game. 4 men, 1 woman, 1 swing

CHUCK
BACHELOR NO. 1
BACHELOR NO. 2
BACHELOR NO. 3
LUCY
ANNOUNCER

7.   The ABC's of Dating
Three young girls date their way through the alphabet only to find that it may better to stick with one good thing then to explore twenty-six. 3 women

LIBBY
CAROLINA
TATI

8.   The Sacrifice of Dating
A couple finds that true love comes at a price when a matchmaker will go to any length to keep her perfect matchmaking record intact. 1 man, 3 women

SEBASTIAN
LESLIE
DARIA
LAURA

9. Natural Dating

Two people with little in common are unwillingly brought together at a nudist colony where the residents observe butterflies. Together they learn that beauty is more than wing deep. 2 men, 1 woman

GEORGE
LESTER
SARA

10. Post Dating

Les, an aging Romeo working in a small town post office, reminisces about past loves to the son of his lost love. 3 men, 1 woman

LES
CHARLIE
BOB
ETHEL

11. Pre-Dating

Although most cavemen are good at hunting and trapping, Nolo is more interested in making art to impress Nala. However, when one piece of art bursts into flames and fire is discovered Nolo realizes that love and art just don't mix. 3 men, 1 woman

NOLO
ARG
CREBO
NALA

12. Dating Service

Looking for Mr. Right? You've come to The Right Place, but it may not be right for everyone. 1 man, 2 women

DANNY
MS. RIGHT
CHARLOTTE

CREATIVE DATING

CHARACTERS

CRYSTAL
MEGAN
JORDAN
MAN ON FLOOR
WOMAN ON FLOOR
POLICEMAN

SETTING

The lobby of a bank. An imaginary teller is at the front of the stage. A few people stand in line. The desk of **JORDAN KRAMER**, *bank manager, sits in the corner. On the desk are papers and a wedding picture.*

(*JORDAN sits at his desk. Several people stand in line for an imaginary bank teller.* CRYSTAL *and* MEGAN *enter casually. They walk around the stage, looking cautiously in every corner. They look through the audience. They see* JORDAN, *whisper to each other briefly, then pull out guns.*)

CRYSTAL. Nobody move! This is a hold up!

MEGAN. Everybody face down on the floor and don't get up.

(*The people in line get down on the floor.* JORDAN *starts to get onto the floor.* MEGAN *speaks to him.*)

Everybody but you.

CRYSTAL. Oh my God, I can't believe you spoke to him.

MEGAN. He is so cute.

(*The girls laugh giddily.*)

JORDAN. My name is Jordan Kramer. I'm the bank manager.

CRYSTAL. He spoke to me. Did you hear that?

MEGAN. He didn't just speak to you. He spoke to both of us. You spoke to both of us, didn't you?

JORDAN. Yes, I was speaking to both of you. Please don't hurt anyone.

MEGAN. Oh, we won't hurt anyone.

(*A man starts to get up off the ground.*)

CRYSTAL. Get your butt back on that ground mister! What do you think this is?

(*The man drops back onto his face.*)

MEGAN. Hey, he's kind of cute.

CRYSTAL. Focus Megan. We're here for a reason.

MEGAN. You're so right and he is hot.

(*JORDAN tries to reach under the desk to trip the alarm.* CRYSTAL *points the gun at him.*)

CRYSTAL. Whoa! Hey! Don't touch that alarm! Like, that is so not cool. Now come around to the front of the desk where we can see you.

(JORDAN *brings his hands up and comes around to the front of the desk. Both of the girls look him over.*)

MEGAN. Oh my God! What a total hottie!

CRYSTAL. Look at him. He's so beautiful. He even knows how to dress.

MEGAN. And so brave. Willing to risk his own life to trip the alarm.

(*The girls squeal.*)

JORDAN. Let's try and resolve this situation quickly.

CRYSTAL. He's talking to me again.

MEGAN. Crystal, he's talking to both of us, remember?

CRYSTAL. Well, I'm one of us which means he's talking to me.

MEGAN. All right, he's talking to you...too.

JORDAN. The safe is locked and on a timer. You won't be able to access it.

CRYSTAL. The safe?

MEGAN. Oh, we don't want the money.

JORDAN. You don't?

CRYSTAL. No. What would we do with the money? I'm sure all of those bills are traceable so even if we tried to spend them we'd just get caught, put in jail and never get another pedicure.

MEGAN. I would die without my pedicures. Please don't talk like that again, Crystal.

CRYSTAL. Sorry Megan.

JORDAN. Well, all of the safety deposit boxes have double-locking devices on them. They're nearly impossible to override.

CRYSTAL. Oh, we don't want those either.

MEGAN. What's in them? Stocks, bonds, jewelry and other

crap like that. No thank you. You should see my house. I have so much crap in there already. I am in serious need of a garage sale.

CRYSTAL. Hey, that's a great idea. We should do one this weekend. The weather is supposed to be so awesome.

MEGAN. You're right. We could make signs and sell lemonade. It would be so much fun.

JORDAN. Excuse me ladies.

CRYSTAL. He's so polite.

MEGAN. What a doll.

JORDAN. Can we get on with this please? I'm sure these people are frightened and would like to go home.

CRYSTAL. Oh, yeah. Sorry to hold you up. We'll be done soon.

MEGAN. We just get so distracted.

JORDAN. I noticed. So you don't want the money or the safety deposit boxes?

MEGAN. No.

JORDAN. Then what do you want?

CRYSTAL. We just want to spend some time with you.

JORDAN. Me?

MEGAN. Uh huh. Get to know you better.

JORDAN. You can't be serious.

CRYSTAL. Oh yes. Very serious.

(*to* MEGAN)

He was only talking to me that time.

MEGAN. You're right. He was only talking to you that time.

JORDAN. Excuse me ladies. What is going on here?

CRYSTAL. He is so hot when he's forceful. Do it again.

JORDAN. What?

CRYSTAL. Say something demanding.

JORDAN. Get out of here you crazy bimbos.

MEGAN. That was really good. I got goosebumps. See.

JORDAN. Look, I don't know what's going on here, but I'm calling the police.

(**MEGAN** *and* **CRYSTAL** *point their guns at* **JORDAN**.)

MEGAN. Hey! Whoa! Stop! Don't make us shoot you. That would really suck.

CRYSTAL. Yeah. Just calm down. Do you want some coffee or juice or something?

JORDAN. No, thank you. I want you to leave.

MEGAN. Well, that's not very nice. Here we are risking our lives just to get to know you better. You could show a little gratitude.

JORDAN. Are you insane? You're robbing my bank so that you can get to know me?

CRYSTAL. We're not really robbing you. I mean, we don't want to take anything. We just thought you were hot and we wanted to talk to you.

JORDAN. You could make an appointment like everyone else.

MEGAN. An appointment for what? It's not like we need a mortgage or anything. We just want a date.

JORDAN. A date? Have you tried Match.com?

MEGAN. Have we tried Match.com? Oh my God, yes.

CRYSTAL. And dating services and speed dating and blind dates. We've tried it all.

MEGAN. And if we had any luck do you think we would be here right now?

JORDAN. Guess not.

CRYSTAL. Look, we don't want to hurt anyone...

(*The man tries to get up again.*)

MEGAN. Buddy, you're starting to make me angry. The next time you get up I'm gonna blow your head off.

MAN. Sorry.

(*He gets back onto the ground.*)

MEGAN. Now, what was I saying? Oh yes, we don't want to hurt anyone. We just want a date with you.

JORDAN. Well this is not exactly my idea of a great first date.

CRYSTAL. Ours either, but we didn't know how else to meet you.

JORDAN. One more time. You're robbing this bank just to get a date with me?

MEGAN. Not robbing it, just delaying business for a little while.

JORDAN. So if I agree to go out with you you'll let everyone go?

CRYSTAL. Well, that's what we wanted to do, but I'm not sure it's a very good idea now.

MEGAN. Why not?

CRYSTAL. What if the people leave and go to the police?

(*Outside a police siren is heard.*)

MEGAN. Oh great. Too late.

(**MEGAN** *reaches into her pocket, takes out her cell phone and dials.*)

Hello Susie. It's Megan. I'm gonna have to cancel my hair appointment this afternoon. I know it's short notice, but I really don't think I'll be able to make it. Reschedule? I may be tied up for a while. I'll call you when I'm free. Bye.

(**MEGAN** *puts the phone back in her pocket.*)

CRYSTAL. You canceled your hair appointment.

MEGAN. God, I am so bummed. Look at these roots. If I don't get them done soon I'm going to look like a skunk.

CRYSTAL. Eww!

MEGAN. Eww!

JORDAN. Listen, why don't you let all these people go and we can work this out alone.

CRYSTAL. Oh my God, he wants to be alone with me.

MEGAN. He wants to be alone with us, Crystal.

(*to* **JORDAN**)

You didn't mean that you just wanted be alone with Crystal, did you?

JORDAN. I...

CRYSTAL. He looked at me when he said that.

MEGAN. But he was talking to both of us.

CRYSTAL. I realize you are in a mood because you had to cancel your hair appointment, but that doesn't give you the right to get snappy with me.

MEGAN. Snappy? Oh God, Crissy, you're so right. I'm so sorry. I love you.

CRYSTAL. I love you too.

(*The girls hug.*)

JORDAN. Um, excuse me?

MEGAN. What do you want?

JORDAN. Well, you're kind of in the middle of robbing a bank.

CRYSTAL. You may be hot, but you're not very bright. How many times do we have to tell you that we're not robbing the bank, just delaying business?

JORDAN. Right.

MEGAN. Besides, this is all your fault anyway.

JORDAN. My fault?

CRYSTAL. He hasn't heard a word we've said. He really isn't very bright, is he? God, I'm so sorry we even bothered with this one. And you missed a hair appointment.

MEGAN. We both thought he was worth it. But you know, Crissy, now that I look at him he's not nearly as hot as I thought he was.

JORDAN. What?

MEGAN. Well, you don't listen and you certainly aren't very polite. You haven't even offered us a chair or a soda or anything since we've been here. What kind of a bank manager are you?

CRYSTAL. I think we should go.

MEGAN. And we should take our accounts with us. This

bank has terrible customer service.

CRYSTAL. Good idea.

MEGAN. We'd like two withdrawal slips please.

JORDAN. What?

MEGAN. Withdrawal slips. We're taking our business some-place else.

JORDAN. Ladies, you don't want to do that. We'd really hate to lose your business.

CRYSTAL. Sorry Jordan. You blew it. We want to take our money and our affection elsewhere.

JORDAN. But...

(*The girls go to* JORDAN*'s desk.*)

MEGAN. No butts. Withdrawal slips please.

(MEGAN *notices a picture on* JORDAN*'s desk.*)

What's this?

JORDAN. A photo.

CRYSTAL. It's a wedding picture.

MEGAN. You're married?

JORDAN. Well, I...

CRYSTAL. Oh my God! I can't believe you! How could you do this to us?

JORDAN. Do what to you?

MEGAN. We go through all of this trouble for you and you don't even have the consideration to tell us you're married?

JORDAN. You're insane.

CRYSTAL. Don't bother with the withdrawal slips. We'll use the ATM. Come on Megan. Let's go.

(*yelling off stage*)

POLICEMAN. You! Inside the bank! Can you hear us?

CRYSTAL. Oh my God! It's the police!

MEGAN. Thank God. Maybe the day's not a total waste. I love men in uniforms.

CRYSTAL. Me too.

(*The girls go to the front of the stage and look out the imaginary windows.*)

The SWAT team is coming! Look at them. They really know how to pile out of that truck.

MEGAN. They're so hot in those uniforms with the little helmets and guns.

CRYSTAL. Do you think they teach them how to look that sexy?

MEGAN. No. You have to be born with a gift like that.

JORDAN. Ladies, perhaps we could...

(MEGAN *points her gun at* JORDAN.)

MEGAN. Why are you talking to me? Can't you see we're busy here?

CRYSTAL. I told you, not too bright.

(*Yelling off stage.*)

POLICEMAN. You! Inside of the bank! Let the hostages go!

MEGAN. Oh my God, I totally forgot about the hostages.

(*Yelling*)

Just a minute!

CRYSTAL. And we were putting Jordan down for being thoughtless. We totally forgot about these poor people on the floor. Here, let me help you up.

(CRYSTAL *and* MEGAN *help people up from the floor.*)

MEGAN. Your clothes are wrinkled. I am so sorry. Let me brush you off.

(*To* WOMAN.)

CRYSTAL. That shirt is way cute. Where did you get it?

WOMAN. Target.

CRYSTAL. Shut up! Like I have not been there in so long because the last time I went there the clothes were like so blah, but this is totally cute. Did they have any other colors?

WOMAN. I think so.

CRYSTAL. I am so there.

(**MEGAN** *helps up* **MAN.**)

MEGAN. Sorry I yelled at you. I'm usually not that volatile, but we all have our moments.

MAN. I understand.

MEGAN. You do?

MAN. Yeah. It must be really tough trying to get a date like this. Of course, I've never tried it, but it sure looks difficult.

MEGAN. You don't know the half of it.

MAN. Listen, I couldn't help but overhear your conversation and I know you were really interested in Mr. Kramer here, but since he's kind of fallen out of favor with you, if you know what I mean, I was wondering if you might like to go out with me sometime?

MEGAN. Aren't you just the sweetest guy in the whole world? Cute too. Sure. I'd love to go out with you. Here's my e-mail.

(**MEGAN** *pulls a card from her pocket and hands it to Man.*)

MAN. Browsing for men at single girls dot com. Great. I'll shoot you an e-mail.

MEGAN. Shoot you an e-mail. That is so funny. Shoot you. Crystal. Crystal, I got a date and he has a sense of humor.

CRYSTAL. You got a date?

(*The girls squeal.*)

WOMAN. Excuse me? Can we go now?

CRYSTAL. Oh my gosh, I'm so sorry. Yes. All of you. Have a nice day. It was really great meeting you. Well, we didn't actually meet, but you were all so well behaved. We really appreciate it.

MEGAN. Yeah. Thanks so much. Bye now.

(*The hostages leave.* **JORDAN** *approaches* **MEGAN** *and* **CRYSTAL**.)

JORDAN. Ladies, I don't know what to say.

MEGAN. Don't say anything Mr. Liar Pants. Just go. You have totally ruined our day. Well, actually, no you haven't. I got a date.

(*The girls squeal.*)

JORDAN. I'll make sure to tell the police how well you treated everyone.

MEGAN. Gee thanks. It's the least you could do. And say hello to your wife for us.

(**JORDAN** *exits.* **POLICE** *enter.*)

POLICEMAN. Put down your weapons and no one gets hurt.

CRYSTAL. Weapons. (*looking at her gun*) Oh my God, I totally forgot we had these. Here you go.

(**CRYSTAL** *hands her gun to the* **POLICEMAN**.)

POLICEMAN. It's a squirt gun.

CRYSTAL. Of course. What, do you think, we're crazy? There is no way you would ever catch me touching a real gun.

MEGAN. We could break a nail or something.

CRYSTAL. Nail? I totally forgot about my nail appointment.

(**CRYSTAL** *takes out her cell phone and dials.*)

Hey Cat, it's Criss. No, I totally did not hear about Jenny. What happened to her? He didn't? She did? Shut up!

POLICEMAN. Um, excuse me, but you're under arrest.

CRYSTAL. Oh, yeah, sorry. I'll just be a minute.

(*on the phone*)

Hey Cat, I'm not going to make it to my nail appointment. I have to go with these policemen. What? I don't know I'll ask.

(*to the police*)

Are any of you single?

(*Several of them raise their hands.*)

There's a few. Sure, I'll try to get numbers. Love you girl. Bye.

(*to the police*)

Thank you so much. If I don't cancel she still charges me.

POLICEMAN. I see. Can we go now?

CRYSTAL. Oh my God, yes. I'm so sorry.

(**POLICEMAN** *starts to put handcuffs on* **MEGAN.**)

MEGAN. Is that really necessary? I bruise kind of easy and I'd hate to look bad for my date.

POLICEMAN. I don't think you'll be giving me any trouble, so I guess I don't have to put these on you.

(**POLICEMAN** *starts to put the handcuffs on* **CRYSTAL.** *Their eyes meet.*)

CRYSTAL. Wow, you have the most beautiful eyes. What color are they?

POLICEMAN. Brown.

CRYSTAL. They're very exotic.

POLICEMAN. Thanks.

CRYSTAL. I couldn't help but notice that you raised your hand when I asked who was single. What are you doing later tonight?

POLICEMAN. What did you have in mind?

CRYSTAL. How about a movie?

POLICEMAN. Sure. I'm always up for a good action flick.

CRYSTAL. Yeah. What time?

POLICEMAN. You could probably be out on bail by seven.

CRYSTAL. Sounds perfect! Would you mind giving me a ride home after you arrest me so I can freshen up? It's been kind of a long day.

POLICEMAN. Sure.

MEGAN. Crissy, you got a date too?

CRYSTAL. Yeah. Isn't that awesome?

(*The girls squeal.*)

MEGAN. Oh my God. And to think we wasted all that time on all those other dating services when all we had to do is rob a bank.

CRYSTAL. Um, Megan, we weren't robbing it.

MEGAN. Oh yeah. I forgot.

(*Lights down.*)

PROPS

Two guns
Two cell phones
A framed wedding photo
Hand cuffs

BLIND DATING

CHARACTERS

JOE
TED
ASHLEY
LAUREN

SETTING

A driving range at a golf course. A tall table and four bar stools are off to one side.

(JOE, ASHLEY *and* TED *are at a golf driving range.* JOE
*is blind and a bit of a klutz. Throughout the play he
knocks things over, runs into things, bumps into people
and is generally very clumsy. He's setting up his shot
with the help of* TED.)

JOE. No!

ASHLEY. Why not?

(JOE *shoots. A car alarm goes off.*)

TED. One eighty five and a Lexus.

JOE. Not again!

ASHLEY. Give this woman a chance. What have you got to
lose?

JOE. A relaxing evening. A little money. My life.

(JOE *trips over something on the ground and falls into*
TED. TED *casually catches him and sets him upright.*)

TED. You make it sound like dating's a bad thing.

JOE. Not dating, blind dating.

(TED *sets up his shot.*)

ASHLEY. You'll really like this girl. I'm sure of it.

TED. My friend said she's perfect for you.

JOE. No!

TED. Come on.

JOE. Not interest Ted.

ASHLEY. Just give her a chance.

JOE. Wait! I smell something funny.

TED. Hey, it wasn't me.

JOE. Cute. You didn't invite this woman to join us, did
you?

TED. I wouldn't do something like that.

JOE. Uh huh.

ASHLEY. But maybe I would.

JOE. Ashley.

(**TED** *shoots.*)

TED. Two thirty five.

ASHLEY. You may like Lauren.

JOE. Lauren?

ASHLEY. She should be here any minute.

(**JOE** *begins to gather his things. As he picks things up he drops them on the ground.* **ASHLEY** *picks them up and puts them back on the table.*)

TED. What are you doing?

JOE. I don't do blind dates.

ASHLEY. Why not?

JOE. I've tried it before. It didn't work out.

TED. It can't be that bad.

JOE. Aside from the fact that my last blind date was as bright as a toothpick, she ended up stalking me for three months.

TED. She stalked you? After one date? You must have made a great first impression.

JOE. She felt sorry for me. She wanted to help me.

ASHLEY. Sounds like her intentions were good.

JOE. Are you kidding? She was a Peace Corp blood sucking vampire. Getting rid of that woman was tougher than going to law school.

ASHLEY. I'm sure Lauren's not like that.

JOE. I'm not taking my chances. I hope you enjoy the company of...

(**LAUREN** *approaches the group led by a Waiter. She is blind and uses cane to find her way.* **JOE** *turns and bumps into her.*)

Excuse me.

LAUREN. I'm sorry.

JOE. It was my fault.

LAUREN. No it was mine. Are you Joe?

JOE. Uh, yes. I am.

LAUREN. Hi. I'm Lauren. Nice to meet you.

JOE. Oh. Hi.

LAUREN. Hi.

ASHLEY. Hi Lauren. We're Ted and Ashley.

LAUREN. Hi.

TED. Glad you could join us.

LAUREN. Me too.

TED. Joe, are you leaving?

JOE. Yes.

ASHLEY. No.

JOE. What?

> (**JOE** *knocks over the golf clubs.* **TED** *casually picks them up.*)

LAUREN. Did I come at the wrong time?

ASHLEY. No, not at all. Joe's not leaving.

LAUREN. Please don't leave on my account.

JOE. Why would I do that?

LAUREN. Because it's a blind date.

JOE. I've got no problem with that.

LAUREN. Are you sure?

JOE. Yeah. Of course. Why would that bother me?

LAUREN. Some people hate blind dates.

JOE. Not me.

LAUREN. Then you're staying?

JOE. Sure. I'm always ready for a good adventure. Who's up?

TED. Lauren, you wanna give it a swing?

LAUREN. Me? I've never golfed before.

TED. Then now is the time to learn.

LAUREN. You think I can?

TED. If Joe can do it, anyone can do it.

JOE. Hey!

LAUREN. All right. I'll give it a try.

ASHLEY. I'll help you. Here, this is a driver.

> (**ASHLEY** *hands* **LAUREN** *a golf club.*)

> Hold the club like this. The ball is here. Pull the club back like this and swing.

> (**LAUREN** *swings and hits the imaginary ball. A window breaks.*)

LAUREN. Did I do that?

TED. No. It was probably someone else. Ashley, you're up.

> (**ASHLEY** *sets up her shot.*)

ASHLEY. So what do you do for a living, Lauren?

LAUREN. I'm a lawyer.

JOE. Me too. Where do you work?

LAUREN. I have my own practice. Labor Law.

JOE. Me too. What's your specialty?

LAUREN. Discrimination.

JOE. Mine too.

LAUREN. What a coincidence.

> (**ASHLEY** *shoots.*)

TED. One seventy five.

ASHLEY. You two have something in common.

JOE. I guess we do.

> (**JOE** *goes to lean on a pole and slips.*)

> How long have you been practicing?

LAUREN. Three years.

JOE. I've been practicing for four. I started out in medical malpractice, but switched to Labor Law about two years ago.

TED. It was the best thing you ever did. Joe, you're up.

JOE. Thanks.

> (**JOE** *sets up his shot with the help of* **TED.**)

LAUREN. What firm did you start at?

JOE. Lawson and Baker.

LAUREN. Lawson and Baker?

JOE. Yes.

LAUREN. They're not the most reputable firm.

JOE. The rumors aren't true.

LAUREN. I've defended against some of their lawyers and they didn't exactly practice by the book.

JOE. Like who?

LAUREN. Frank Peterson.

JOE. Frank's a hell of a lawyer.

(**JOE** *swings and a woman screams.*)

TED. Nice! Two hundred and Mrs. Kenderbott.

JOE. (*yelling*) Sorry Mrs. Kenderbott!

LAUREN. Frank is a snake. He called my co-counsel a boy scout with a stick up his ass because he insisted on following the local rules.

JOE. Maybe he thought the local rules didn't apply in that case.

LAUREN. What do you mean they didn't apply? They're the rules of the court.

JOE. Yeah, but who says that they need to be followed precisely?

LAUREN. You're joking?

JOE. Well...

(**JOE** *makes a hand gesture. The golf club flies from his hand into the wings and breaks some dishes.*)

TED. Uh, Lauren, can I get you a drink? The service here is a bit slow.

LAUREN. Yes. Thanks. Gin and tonic with a dash of bitters.

JOE. I'll go with you. To help.

TED. No need.

JOE. I want to. Be right back.

(**JOE** *and* **TED** *exit.*)

ASHLEY. Why don't we have a seat and wait for the drinks?

LAUREN. Sure.

ASHLEY. Joe's passionate about being a lawyer.

LAUREN. Obviously.

ASHLEY. He's worked hard to get to where he's at.

LAUREN. We all have.

ASHLEY. Lawson and Baker fired him.

LAUREN. What? Then why was he just defending them?

ASHLEY. It's complicated. Just trust me, Joe's a good guy. Don't hold it against him that he worked for LB.

LAUREN. All right. Why'd they fire him?

ASHLEY. You should probably ask him that question.

LAUREN. Of course. Thanks for telling me.

ASHLEY. I didn't want you to think he was jerk.

LAUREN. Fair enough. So what do you do, Ashley?

ASHLEY. I'm an ophthalmologist

LAUREN. I've seen a lot of those in my life. Well, not really seen them, but you know what I mean.

ASHLEY. Funny.

LAUREN. As a blind lawyer it's necessary to have a good sense of humor.

ASHLEY. I bet.

LAUREN. You think lawyer jokes are bad, blind lawyer jokes are worse.

ASHLEY. Blind lawyer jokes? You have to tell one when Joe gets back. He'll love it.

LAUREN. All right. So how do you know Joe?

ASHLEY. Through work. He's a patient of mine.

(**JOE** *and* **TED** *enter with drinks.*)

JOE. Here you are ladies.

(**JOE** *hands the drink to* **LAUREN,** *but he fumbles the glass and the drink spills.*)

Oh no! I'm sorry!

LAUREN. It's okay.

JOE. It's not okay.

LAUREN. It was my fault.

JOE. No, it was my fault.

(ASHLEY *helps* LAUREN *wipe her clothes.*)

LAUREN. It's all right. You saved me the trouble of spilling it on myself later.

JOE. You probably think I did it on purpose.

LAUREN. The thought hadn't crossed my mind, but now that you mention it...

JOE. I didn't.

ASHLEY. He wouldn't do that.

LAUREN. It's really nothing. Just forget about it.

JOE. Maybe I should go.

LAUREN. Why?

JOE. This isn't exactly going well.

TED. No you don't. Stay and finish your beer.

JOE. I've already made an ass out of myself twice.

LAUREN. Don't be a coward. Stay.

JOE. Did you just call me a coward?

LAUREN. If the shoe fits.

JOE. I am not a coward!

(JOE *accidentally bumps the table.*)

Clumsy, but not a coward.

LAUREN. Then why are you running away?

JOE. I'm not. I'm staying.

LAUREN. Good. I'm glad.

JOE. Me too.

LAUREN. Fine.

JOE. Fine.

(JOE *sits.*)

TED. So.

JOE. So.

ASHLEY. So how about a joke? Lauren knows a lot of great lawyer jokes. Why don't you tell us one of your jokes, Lauren?

LAUREN. Okay. I'll tell you my favorite. One morning a blind bunny was hopping down the bunny trail and he tripped and fell over a large snake.

JOE. A blind bunny?

LAUREN. Yes and he says, "Please excuse me! I didn't mean to trip over you, but I'm blind and can't see." The snake says, "That's all right. I didn't mean to trip you, but I'm blind too, and I didn't see you coming."

JOE. Let me get this straight, we have a blind snake and a blind bunny?

LAUREN. That's right. So the snake says, "By the way, what kind of animal are you?" The bunny says, "I don't know. I'm blind. I've never seen myself. Maybe you could examine me and find out." So the snake feels the bunny and says, "You're soft, cuddly, have long ears, a fluffy tail and a twitchy little nose... You must be a bunny rabbit!" The bunny says, "Thanks. By the way, what kind of animal are you?" The snake says, "I don't know." So the bunny feels the snake and says, "You're hard, cold, slimy and you haven't got any balls. You must be a lawyer."

(*Everyone laughs but* **JOE**.)

JOE. Payback for spilling your drink?

LAUREN. Excuse me?

JOE. A blind lawyer joke.

LAUREN. Joe, I'm sorry. I've never taken any lawyer jokes personally. I thought you wouldn't either.

JOE. It's hard enough being a blind lawyer without people making fun of you.

LAUREN. I wasn't making fun of you. I was...wait, Joe, are you blind?

JOE. No. I just carry the walking stick as a fashion statement.

(**LAUREN** *laughs.*)

You think that's funny?

LAUREN. Yes.

ASHLEY. You didn't know?

LAUREN. No, and from the sounds of it Joe doesn't know either.

JOE. Know what?

TED. What's going on here?

ASHLEY. Of course. We didn't tell him so how else would he know?

JOE. What? Know what? What the hell are you people talking about!

LAUREN. Joe, I'm blind too.

JOE. You're blind?

LAUREN. Yes. I wasn't telling that joke to make fun of you. I was making fun of myself.

JOE. You are? You were? You did?

LAUREN. I am, I was and I did.

JOE. Ted?

TED. She's blind.

JOE. Idiot strike three.

ASHLEY. It's not your fault. We should have told you Lauren is blind.

JOE. You're right. I'm blind, not psychic. How am I supposed to know she's blind if I can't see her?

ASHLEY. Right. Sorry.

(**LAUREN** *laughs again.*)

JOE. Glad you think it's funny.

LAUREN. It is. It kind of redefines the meaning of a blind date, doesn't it?

JOE. Yeah. It does, doesn't it. Can we start over?

LAUREN. Sure. Hi. My name is Lauren and I'm a blind lawyer.

JOE. Hi. My name is Joe and I'm a blind lawyer.

TED. I feel like I'm in lawyers anonymous.

ASHLEY. You are. Ted's a lawyer too.

LAUREN. A blind lawyer?

JOE. No, but a damn fine lawyer anyway.

(**JOE** *slaps* **TED** *on the back as he's taking a drink of his beer.*)

TED. You say that about all your friends.

JOE. Yeah, but I don't pay all of my friends to represent me.

LAUREN. Represent you? What type of case?

JOE. Discrimination.

LAUREN. My favorite type. Suing anyone I'd know?

JOE. Lawson and Baker.

LAUREN. Wait! You're suing Lawson and Baker for discrimination?

JOE. That's right.

LAUREN. But you said they were a great firm.

JOE. I didn't say that. I said that Frank Peterson was a great lawyer, which he is, snake or no snake.

LAUREN. I'm sorry I called him that.

TED. Why? He is a snake.

LAUREN. But you were defending him?

JOE. I had to make sure you weren't one of their spies.

LAUREN. Okay, now I'm really lost. Why would they send a spy to have a date with you?

TED. They're trying to prove that Joe isn't blind.

LAUREN. What?

JOE. Two years ago the flat screen TV in the Lawson and Baker conference room came loose from the wall and hit me on the head. I've been blind ever since.

LAUREN. That's terrible, but what does that have to do with discrimination?

TED. When they found out that Joe would never regain his sight they fired him.

LAUREN. That's discrimination.

JOE. They said I could no longer do the job I was hired for. Not discrimination.

LAUREN. But you have your own practice proving them wrong.

JOE. Yes, so their only defense is to show that I'm not blind so they can say they fired me for incompetence.

LAUREN. That's crazy.

ASHLEY. And so they won't have to pay the medical bills and the negligence lawsuit.

LAUREN. They're coming from all sides.

JOE. Rotten, huh?

ASHLEY. It's bad enough that Joe lost his sight and his job, but the fact that LB doesn't want to compensate him is just screwed.

LAUREN. I can only imagine what you've been going through.

JOE. It's been hard. But enough about me. Who's ready to drive?

(**JOE** *grabs a golf club and hits a chair, knocking it over.* **JOE** *casually picks up the chair.*)

ASHLEY. It's Lauren's turn.

LAUREN. I'll pass.

TED. Not a chance. Let the master help you this time.

(**TED** *sets up a ball and places the driver in* **LAUREN**'s *hand.*)

A little more this way. The ball is here. Pull back, everyone watch out and swing!

(**LAUREN** *swings and a cat screeches.*)

LAUREN. Oops!

JOE. Don't worry about it. I do it all the time. Ashley, you're up.

(**ASHLEY** *sets up her shot.*)

ASHLEY. Lauren, did you start at a big firm too?

LAUREN. No. Always had my own practice.

JOE. How long have you been blind?

LAUREN. My whole life.

JOE. I can't imagine doing law school blind. It was tough enough being able to see.

LAUREN. It wasn't easy.

(*A cell phone rings.* **LAUREN** *pulls the phone from her purse.*)

Hello. Yes. Oh yes. Can you hold a moment please? Thank you.

(*She covers the phone with her hand*)

Would you excuse me for a minute? It's a client.

JOE. Sure.

(**LAUREN** *walks to the edge of the stage and talks on the phone.*)

Lauren's nice.

TED. And cute.

ASHLEY. And fake.

JOE. What?

(**ASHLEY** *swings.*)

ASHLEY. She's not blind.

TED. Are you sure?

ASHLEY. Pretty sure.

TED. How do you know?

ASHLEY. Her eyes reacted when Joe spilled the drink on her shirt and again when her phone rang.

JOE. Lawson and Baker?

TED. Good guess.

JOE. What should we do this time?

TED. Sodium pentothal.

JOE. It won't hurt her, will it?

ASHLEY. No. If anything it'll put her to sleep for a few minutes at the most.

JOE. Okay.

(**ASHLEY** *pulls out a small bottle filled with powder. She looks around, then carefully pours some into* **LAUREN***'s drink.* **LAUREN** *walks back to the table.*)

LAUREN. Sorry about that. What were we talking about?

JOE. I'm not sure, but I'd like to propose a toast to my date.

(**JOE** *raises his glass.*)

You've been a real sport.

LAUREN. Thank you.

JOE. Let me help you, Lauren.

(**JOE** *reaches for* **LAUREN***'s glass and it teeters a bit.*)

LAUREN. I've got it, thanks.

(**LAUREN** *picks up her glass.*)

JOE. Cheers!

ASHLEY. Cheers!

TED. Cheers!

LAUREN. Cheers!

(*They drink.*)

JOE. Who's turn is it?

(**LAUREN** *gets a strange look on her face.*)

ASHLEY. Lauren, is something wrong?

LAUREN. I'm feeling a little dizzy.

ASHLEY. It's working.

TED. Lauren, do you work for Lawson & Baker?

LAUREN. No. I would never work for those crooks.

ASHLEY. Lauren, are you blind?

LAUREN. Yes.

ASHLEY. Completely?

LAUREN. I can see shadows.

ASHLEY. Uh oh.

JOE. Ashley?

ASHLEY. I didn't think about that.

LAUREN. I wanted to thank you for the drink and for teaching me how to golf. You're all so sweet. Joe, you're really a nice guy and I hope we can go out again.

JOE. I am? You do?

LAUREN. Yes.

(**LAUREN** *faints.*)

JOE. Oh great! My first nice date in almost a year and we knock her out.

TED. And she's not working for LB.

ASHLEY. Okay. So I made a mistake. She'll be all right. The effects only last a few minutes and there shouldn't be any side effects.

JOE. And when she wakes up what are we going to tell her? Sorry, we thought you were one of the bad guys so we drugged you to find out?

TED. Guess we'll have to.

JOE. I can't believe this.

(**LAUREN** *wakes.*)

LAUREN. What happened?

JOE. Lauren, are you okay?

LAUREN. I think so. What happened to me?

JOE. Idiot strike number four.

LAUREN. What?

ASHLEY. You said you were blind, but I saw your eyes react when the drink spilled on you and thought you were lying. I didn't know you could see shadows.

LAUREN. I don't understand.

TED. We thought you were working for Lawson and Baker so we gave you sodium pentothal.

LAUREN. Truth serum?

ASHLEY. Yes. We're really sorry.

JOE. We're more than sorry. Can you forgive us?

TED. And don't sue us.

> (**LAUREN** *laughs.*)

LAUREN. This is by far the most exciting date I've ever been on.

JOE. It is?

LAUREN. There's no way you'll be able to top this.

JOE. Top it?

LAUREN. On our next date.

JOE. You want to go out with me again?

LAUREN. Only if you promise not to drug me.

JOE. I promise. Are you free tomorrow? We could go sky diving.

LAUREN. How about we just go out to dinner.

JOE. Okay. I'll drive.

> (*Lights out.*)

PROPS

Golf club
Four glasses
Small vial of sodium pentothal
Two walking sticks for the blind
Cell phone

INTERNET DATING

CHARACTERS

JANIE

JEFF

GEORGE

JULIE

STEVE

HARRISON GREGORY

SETTING

An open room with five desks. On each desk is a keyboard and an imaginary computer. A sign on the wall reads "Internet Dating Seminar Today."

(*JANIE*, *JEFF*, *GEORGE*, *JULIE* *and* *STEVE* *each sit at a desk with a keyboard looking at their computers.*)

JANIE. Hot Insatiable Italian Stallion Insatiably Passionate for Ultimate Unlimited Whirlwind Adventurous Romantic Rendezvous. Huh?

JEFF. Domestic Goddess Seeks Prince Charming. That's me sugar.

GEORGE. Paramecia Need Not Respond. What's a paramecia?

JULIE. My Words Are Cold And Flat...and You? Does he want to know if I'm cold and flat?

STEVE. Why am I doing this?

JANIE. Aztec Warrior Looking For Aztec Queen. Ooh! He has a huge spear!

GEORGE. Eat Dessert First. A woman after my own heart.

JEFF. Beach Beauty Looking to Be Swept Away. She looks just like Jessica Simpson. Wait, that is Jessica Simpson.

STEVE. Okay. Maybe just one little search.

JULIE. Mad scientist seeks brainy female assistant to join sinister plot to conquer the universe.

JANIE. Experience in Scrabble may prove useful. Bonus points if you can program my Tivo.

GEORGE. Looking for an English-speaking man. Hey, I can speak English.

JULIE. Simple Guy Seeking Simple Gal.

JEFF. Smart Woman Seeking Smart Man.

JANIE. Strong Man Wanting Strong Woman.

GEORGE. Raggedy Ann Missing Raggedy Andy.

STEVE. Primeval Love Goddess Waiting to Conquer Your Heart.

JANIE. I just want to find a decent guy.

GEORGE. I just want to find a nice girl.

JULIE. Someone who's looking for love.

JEFF. Children are optional.

STEVE. I can't do this.

JANIE. Entertaining.

JEFF. Compelling.

JULIE. Addicting.

GEORGE. Frustrating.

STEVE. Terrifying.

> (**HARRISON GREGORY,** *a small man with glasses, walks out of the wings and stands in front of the group.*)

HARRISON. Hello daters. My name is Harrison Gregory. Sometimes I'm referred to as The Love Guru.

JEFF. You're The Love Guru?

HARRISON. Love comes in all shapes and sizes.

STEVE. Excuse me?

HARRISON. Yes?

STEVE. May I go to the bathroom?

HARRISON. Of course. Next time you don't have to raise your hand.

STEVE. Thank you.

> (**STEVE** *rushes out of the room.*)

JEFF. There's no way this guy knows about women.

HARRISON. But I do know about women, Mr. Harting.

JEFF. How did you know my name?

HARRISON. A good guess. If you read my book, "Looking for Love With All the Right Engines" you'd know that Internet love is not based on appearance. That's why it's the most prolific form of dating today.

JEFF. You can't tell me that looks don't matter.

HARRISON. They do, but mostly for people like you, Mr. Harting and you are in the minority. Tell me, why are you here?

JEFF. To meet women.

HARRISON. Then you're in the wrong place. There are only two women here.

JEFF. To meet women on the Internet.

HARRISON. Then you're in the right place because woman

on the Internet want something very specific in a man, something that I can teach you.

JEFF. Sex from you? I don't think so.

HARRISON. A relationship cannot exist simply on sex.

(**STEVE** *walks into the room.*)

STEVE. Sex? Did you say sex? I can't talk about sex.

(**STEVE** *goes to exit.*)

HARRISON. Mr. Brown, please come in and take a seat.

STEVE. I need to use the bathroom.

HARRISON. You just used the bathroom.

STEVE. I forgot something.

HARRISON. What?

STEVE. I don't know.

(**STEVE** *goes to exit again.* **HARRISON** *follows him and brings him back into the room.*)

HARRISON. Please, Mr. Brown. Give me a chance to enrich your life with love.

STEVE. I don't need love. I have an XBox.

HARRISON. We all need love Mr. Brown. Now, please, have a seat.

STEVE. Do I have to?

HARRISON. Yes.

(**STEVE** *sits.*)

Where was I? Oh yes, Internet relationships are more successful than any other form of dating in the world.

JANIE. Why?

HARRISON. Because Ms. Stone, the daters have the opportunity to learn about each other without being inhibited by the physical awkwardness of other types of dating.

JEFF. But what about sex?

HARRISON. Sex is important, but not as important as other things to most Internet daters.

JEFF. No way!

HARRISON. The physical body will eventually fade and what is left is the essence of the relationship. If the relationship is based only on sex, there will be no essence left to carry the relationship.

JULIE. If Internet relationships aren't based on appearance, does that mean we don't have to take our pictures today?

HARRISON. I'm afraid you still have to take your picture. Although looks are not everything they are part of the revelation of who you are.

GEORGE. Oh no.

HARRISON. You don't feel confident with who you are, Mr. Schmidt?

GEORGE. No.

HARRISON. Why not?

GEORGE. Because I don't look like Mr. Harting over there.

HARRISON. But you're an exceptional human being. Why should you worry about how you look?

JEFF. Because that's what women worry about.

JANIE. That is so shallow!

JULIE. And stupid!

HARRISON. And wrong Mr. Harting, but the only way you'll understand is through learning. Let's get started.

GEORGE. This is exciting. What do we do first.

HARRISON. First you need to create a profile. Be honest with who you are and what you're looking for in a mate.

(*Typing.*)

JANIE. Lonely woman seeking man to brighten her days and comfort her nights. Non-smokers only please.

(*Typing.*)

GEORGE. If you like Saturday afternoon naps and Sundays watching football, I'm your man.

(*Typing.*)

JULIE. Tidy, well-groomed girl seeking man to compliment her mannerisms. Must be tall, dark and handsome. Okay, just breathing would do.

(*Typing.*)

JEFF. Handsome, intelligent, sexy man seeks woman to worship him. I hope I don't get any weirdos.

STEVE. Um...um...

(**STEVE** *lays his head on his keyboard.*)

HARRISON. Let me help you, Mr. Brown. Brilliant engineer seeking a one for his zero.

STEVE. How did you know I was an engineer?

HARRISON. Because you exude the knowledge and command of a language that is only found in a computer engineer.

STEVE. I exude?

HARRISON. You do exude.

STEVE. Wow! I exude!

(**STEVE** *types.*)

HARRISON. Now, your profile should be set to searchable so that others can see who you are.

GEORGE. Do we have to?

HARRISON. Yes, Mr. Schmidt. The women of the world are looking for you.

GEORGE. What women?

HARRISON. You'll find out by setting your profile to searchable. Next we need to take your picture so your potential date can see your brilliance shine through in your face.

(**HARRISON** *takes out a digital camera.*)

GEORGE. My brilliance?

HARRISON. Yes, Mr. Schmidt. Your brilliant eyes, your brilliant smile.

GEORGE. My brilliant appetite?

HARRISON. If that's what you want your picture convey, then it will come through.

GEORGE. Then snap away. Sirloin!!

(**HARRISON** *takes a picture of* **GEORGE.**)

JULIE. I hate pictures.

HARRISON. With such exceptional inner beauty you should be ashamed of yourself for wishing to hide it from the world.

JULIE. I should?

HARRISON. Yes, you should. You're lovely and you share that loveliness with a smile.

(**HARRISON** *takes a picture of* **JULIE.**)

JEFF. I'm an internationally known model. You'll have to call my agent to get a release.

HARRISON. Already done. Smile.

(**HARRISON** *takes a picture of* **JEFF.**)

JEFF. You're kidding, right? You didn't really call my agent and tell him I'm doing this dating seminar, did you? I mean, if he knew...

HARRISON. No, Mr. Harting, I didn't call your agent. The release was on the registration form.

JEFF. Oh. Yeah, well it's not like I'm ashamed of doing this or anything.

HARRISON. Of course not. I understand.

JANIE. I'm not sure I agree with you that pictures are necessary for the Internet dating process.

HARRISON. You don't have to agree with me, Ms. Stone, but for the sake of this seminar it's required of all students to have their photograph placed on their profile.

JANIE. Oh, well, I suppose I can do it if it's part of the educational format.

(**JANIE** *smiles stiffly.*)

HARRISON. Relax Ms. Stone.

JANIE. I can't.

HARRISON. Let me help you. Did you have a pet as a child?

JANIE. Yes. A black and white cat named Bandit.

HARRISON. I'm sure he was cute.

JANIE. He was adorable. He was white with this little black mask around his eyes.

(**HARRISON** *snaps the picture.*)

HARRISON. Thank you, Ms. Stone.

JANIE. But...

HARRISON. Hello Mr. Brown.

STEVE. I don't know why I'm here.

HARRISON. For the same reason everyone else is here - to find love.

STEVE. I'm not good with girls.

HARRISON. I was once like you Mr. Brown, shy and withdrawn, but thanks to the Internet my life is now filled with love and joy.

STEVE. I can't be like you. You're so confident.

HARRISON. I haven't always been confident. Believe in yourself and you too can find happiness.

STEVE. Believe in myself. I can't. I can't. I can't date.

HARRISON. Yes you can. Think of a women as a video game controller. They're beautiful, sleek, comfortable to hold and when you push the right buttons, you find love.

STEVE. Wow! That is so deep.

(**HARRISON** *snaps* **STEVE**'s *picture.*)

HARRISON. Now that I have all of your photos I'll upload them to your profiles. In the meantime, I encourage you to browse the profiles of others and even respond to an ad or two. Perhaps you'll find someone that interests you.

(**HARRISON** *goes to the desk in the corner and begins downloading photos onto a computer.*)

(*Reading*)

JANIE. Dear Santa. All I want for Christmas is the woman of my dreams. Please may I have her under my Christmas tree?

(*typing*)

Dear Dear Santa. Have you been a good boy this year? Signed Janie the Elf.

(*reading*)

JEFF. I'm a twenty-four year old extremist looking for my matching puzzle piece. I am driven, gung-ho, confident, intelligent, articulate, punctual, reliable and responsible. If you think you'll bore me, don't bother to respond. If you can handle the action, ping away. Signed Kick Ass 24.

(*writing*)

Dear Kick-Ass. Think you can handle it? Signed Sheer Perfection.

(*reading*)

JULIE. Twenty-eight, six foot four, Latino with a romantic nature. Seeking serious woman for moonlit nights on my yacht.

(*to herself*)

Romantic and rich.

(*typing*)

Dear Romantic Latino. Look no further. I'm the girl for you. Signed Jewel of the Nile.

(*reading*)

GEORGE. Nice German girl seeks American man who loves good cooking. Bratwurst and sauerkraut are my specialties. Yum!

(*typing*))

Hello Frauline. German food is my favorite. I can roast a mean Sauerbraten. Do you Schnitzel? Signed Curious George.

(**HARRISON** *walks around the room looking over shoulders.*)

(**STEVE** *reads.*)

STEVE. Hot, luscious, vibrant redhead looking for a submissive playmate. Signed Flame of Desire.

(*typing*)

Dear Flame of Desire. I...I...I...don't know what to write.

HARRISON. You can do it. Be one with the controller.

STEVE. I am one with the controller.

HARRISON. Good.

JANIE. I got a response!

HARRISON. Good for you. Read it carefully. If you find him interesting, begin a conversation. If not, use the delete key and keep looking. There are thousands of men waiting to hear from you.

(*reading*)

JANIE. Dear Janie the Elf. I have been a very naughty boy. How about you? Are you naughty too? Signed Dear Santa.

(*to herself*)

Loser. Delete.

HARRISON. Try again.

(*reading*)

JEFF. Hello Handsome. Nice ad. Here are some pictures of me. I am a trapeze contortionist with the circus. These photos were taken in the circus stable. Call me if you like what you see.

(*looking closely at the pictures*)

No way. These had to be Photoshopped.

HARRISON. Those are real. In fact, she's rather famous among the Internet dating community.

JEFF. Maybe I should go for it then?

(*pointing at the picture*)

HARRISON. Not unless you have a passion for animals.

JEFF. I think I'll pass.

(*reading*)

JULIE. Dear Jewel of the Nile. Thank you for your e-mail. Although I like your pictures, I don't think you're really my type. Good luck with your man hunt. Signed Romantic Latino.

(*to herself*)

God, I hate rejection.

HARRISON. At least he had the courtesy to write back.

JULIE. I guess.

HARRISON. Chin up. You can't expect to find Mr. Right after one e-mail. Keep trying.

(*reading*)

GEORGE. Dear Curious George. I do Schnitzel and Apfel-pfannkuchen. Would you like to meet for a meal? Signed Brunhilda Gunda Irmtraud.

(*typing*)

Dear Brunhilda. I'll bring the meat if you bring the pudding. When and where? Your faithful cook. Curious George. PS - I have attached an old family recipe for warm apple and cabbage slaw. Enjoy!

HARRISON. Mr. Schmidt, it seems you've been lucky enough to find someone with a common interest.

GEORGE. She's pretty too. Look.

HARRISON. Lovely. Good luck!

(*reading*)

STEVE. Dear Steve, if that's your real name. What a great sense of humor! Those pictures you sent were hilarious. Where did you find them? On YouTube? Signed Flame of Desire.

(*typing*)

Dear Flame of Desire. The pictures were from my high school graduation. I'm glad you enjoyed them. I have attached some more pictures. These are from band camp. I'm the guy with the tuba. Hope you like them. Signed Steve.

HARRISON. Congratulations on starting a conversation with Flame of Desire. She's a lovely girl who seems to be truly interested in the real you.

STEVE. I can't believe it! It's exciting!

(*reading*)

JULIE. Younger guy looking for older woman. Older guy looking for younger woman. Younger woman looking for older woman and younger guy.

(*to herself*)

I can't even find one person, let alone two.

HARRISON. Patience Ms. Jones.

(*reading*)

JANIE. Looking for lean, anxious, intellectual types. Addicted to sex, quality distractions, unrealistic expectations and illegal thinking. I'm a charming cynic with a pathological addiction to kamikaze women and the sheer luck to survive them. Yours truly. Alienated.

(*to herself*)

Hmm.

HARRISON. Interested?

JANIE. Maybe a little.

HARRISON. Then what do you have to lose. Send him an e-mail.

JANIE. He could be a bit much for me.

HARRISON. You'll never know until you try.

JANIE. I'll try.

(*reading*)

GEORGE. Dear Curious George. Thank you for the recipe and invitation for dinner. How about next Saturday? Come to my place around eight. The address is below. Your little frauline. Brunhilda.

(*to himself*)

Wunderbar! I've got a date!

JEFF. You're kidding?

HARRISON. Congratulations Mr. Schmidt!

JULIE. That's great, George.

STEVE. You're my idol.

JANIE. We're proud of you George.

HARRISON. However, just because you have a date it doesn't mean your work is done. You have one week to get to know more about this woman so you will be fully prepared to meet her face to face. Keep up the e-mail contact, perhaps get a phone number and an IM login.

GEORGE. I've got a date! A real date!

(*reading*)

STEVE. Dear Steve. What an imagination! Your pictures were so cute. What other surprises do you have for me? Signed your Flame of Desire.

(*to himself*)

She likes me. Harrison, she likes me! What do I do now?

HARRISON. Write her back. Offer to meet her.

STEVE. In person? Oh, I couldn't do that.

HARRISON. Then think of another way to get to know her.

STEVE. I've got it.

(*typing*)

Dear Flame of Desire. I will be on Runescape at 10:35 Pacific Standard Time tonight. Meet me in world 24 by the river and we can trade runes. My online name is DragonSlayer 1454. PS - I have a Santa hat. Signed Steve.

(*to himself*)

That should impress her.

HARRISON. Very creative, Mr. Brown.

(*reading*)

JULIE. I'm a hard working guy. I like to live hard and laugh a lot and run around causing mischief. Do you want to cause mischief with me? Mischief Maker.

(*typing*)

Dear Mischief Maker. You sound like lots of fun. I've attached my photos. Look forward to hearing from you. Signed Jewel of the Nile.

(*to herself*)

Please don't reject me. Please don't reject me.

HARRISON. In life we don't get what we want, we get in life what we are.

JULIE. Huh?

HARRISON. Rejection builds character. Farrah Gray, teen-age billionaire.

JULIE. I need character.

(*reading*)

JEFF. I'm a down to earth woman looking for that special someone. I'm open minded, love to travel, and like to be exposed to new and different things.

(*to himself*)

Me too.

(*reading*)

I have a good sense of humor and love to laugh. Life is what you make of it and I am all about living life.

(*to himself*)

She'll be so easy.

(*typing*)

Dear Sandy. I, too, am down to earth and looking for someone to share adventures with. Attached are my photos from my last modeling job in Peru. Hope you like them. Signed Sheer Perfection.

HARRISON. Mr. Harting, you haven't learned a thing today, have you?

JEFF. Sure I have. I learned that you have to be mushy and down to earth in order to get laid.

HARRISON. You only have to be mushy and down to earth if that's who you really are. Perhaps it would be more effective to be yourself?

JEFF. I am being myself. Using any means I can to get women.

(*reading*)

JANIE. Hot plate, order up!

(*to herself*)

This is silly. There's got to be a decent man out there somewhere.

HARRISON. Don't give up, Janie. You simply have to weed through the bad to find the good.

(*reading*)

STEVE. Dear Steve. I don't know what Runescape is and or what runes are, but if you tell me how to get there I'll meet you tonight. Bet you look cute in a Santa hat. Signed Flame of Desire.

(*to himself*)

I have a date! I have a date!

JEFF. Not you too!

STEVE. Yes! Me too!

HARRISON. See what happens when you put yourself out there.

STEVE. Thank you, Mr. Love Guru! Thank you!

HARRISON. Your welcome, Mr. Brown.

(*typing*)

GEORGE. My Dearest Little Frauline. Would you be interested in going to the polka fair? Buller, Horst And The Melodies will be playing and I'm sure they'll play Hab Ich Dir Heute Schone Gesagt Das Ich Dich Liebe. Your Sauerkraut, Curious George.

HARRISON. The Melodies are very hip.

GEORGE. They're my favorites.

(*reading*)

JULIE. Dear Jewel of the Nile. I'm thinking of robbing a bank this weekend and know you would look great in one of those tight black jumpsuits. Are you in? Signed Mischief Maker.

(*to herself*)

Should I call the police or should I go on the date? I haven't had a date in a while.

HARRISON. How many dates would you get in prison?

JULIE. I'll call 911.

(*browsing on the computer*)

JEFF. Not you. Not you. Not you. Whoa! Who is this beauty queen?

(*reading*)

I am madly in love with myself and have hired someone to throw rose petals in my path. I primp and I love to wear cute clothes. I'll let you change lanes in front of me, but only if I'm busy putting on make-up while driving, talking on my cell phone and drinking a mocha. I fluently speak English, French, German, Italian, Spanish, Portuguese, Dutch, Chinese, Japanese, Arabic, Russian, Hebrew, Hindi, Tagalog, and Urdu. Can you beat that?

(*to himself*)

Wow!

(*typing*)

Dear Sparkle. I am perfect in every way. Nothing more needs to be said. Attached are the photos from my shoot last month in Prague. E-mail me if you like what you see and think you can handle it. Signed Sheer Perfection.

HARRISON. She looks perfect for you. Good luck!

JEFF. I won't need any luck.

(*reading*)

JANIE. Dear Janie the Elf. Thank you for your e-mail. I, too, love dogs, hiking, camping, reading, going to the movies and picnics on the beach. You didn't mention if you like children. I have a two-year old daughter that's very sweet. Would you be interested in talking some more? Signed Realtor Bob.

(*to herself*)

A nice guy. Yes!

HARRISON. He sounds like a good one.

JANIE. He does.

JULIE. I think I've got a good one too. Come here and look at this.

(*reading*)

Dear Jewel of the Nile. You are a true beauty. Your eyes reflect the soul of one who has suffered much, but deserves love. My name is Stan and I'm an archeologist. Would you be interested in meeting me for afternoon tea sometime? Signed Dirt Digger.

(*to* **HARRISON**)

Do you think he's for real?

HARRISON. Only one way to find out.

(*reading*)

JEFF. Dear Sheer Perfection. Your cocky attitude shows me that you're shallow and vein. May I recommend you read the book "Looking for Love With All the Right Engines." It should give you insight about being honest with yourself and others. Then maybe you can find true love on the Internet. Best of Luck. Sparkle.

HARRISON. Rejection is a difficult thing to bear.

JEFF. Yeah. Especially when you're not used to it.

HARRISON. Why did you come here, Jeff?

JEFF. To meet women.

HARRISON. Why did you really come here?

JEFF. I was tired of woman who wanted to be with me just for my looks.

HARRISON. Good, then start over. Forget about how you look and reach into your soul. Now, write your profile based on what you really want from a woman and a relationship.

(*typing*)

JEFF. Hi. My name is Jeff and I'm looking for someone who will like me for who I am and not what I look like. I'm a model and my whole life I've skated by on my looks, but I want something more. If there's a woman out there that can see past the outside to find the good inside, please e-mail me. I could use an honest friend. Signed Humble Jeff.

HARRISON. A plus. Class dismissed.

PROPS

Six computer keyboards
One laptop
Camera

SPEED DATING

CHARACTERS

MAN A

MAN B

MAN C

WOMAN A

WOMAN B

WOMAN C

GUARD

SETTING

A speed dating session. There are three bistro tables with two chairs at each table.

(*The stage is dark.* **MAN B, MAN D** *and* **MAN F** *are seated at the tables. The three women enter stage left and wait. A bell rings and the three women rush to the chairs. A pool of light comes up on* **WOMAN A** *and* **MAN B**.)

MAN B. Hi.

WOMAN A. Hi.

MAN B. Listen, I know we're not supposed to give out any personal information, but I noticed you earlier and I'd like to get to know you. Here's my name and number.

(**MAN B** *hands* **WOMAN A** *a piece of paper. She pushes it back to him.*)

WOMAN A. No thank you. Let's just follow the rules.

(*referring to her list*)

Question Number One: If you could be any farm animal, what would you be?

MAN B. Farm animal?

WOMAN A. Yes. If you could be any farm animal, what would you be?

MAN B. I don't know. I'm from Brooklyn.

WOMAN A. Oh, that's great. You just answered Question Number Four. Can you please answer the questions in order? What farm animal would you be?

MAN B. I don't know. I guess I'd be one of those big rams that climb up the mountains.

WOMAN A. A ram is not a farm animal. If it climbs up the side of a mountain it can't be a farm animal.

MAN B. It could be on a farm on the side of a mountain. I'm sure they have those somewhere.

WOMAN A. I don't think so, but we only have five minutes so I guess I'll have to take it as your answer. Question Number Two: If aliens came from outer space and wanted to take you to their planet, would you go?

MAN B. It depends on the aliens.

WOMAN A. What?

MAN B. I mean, are they freaky looking things with tentacles that want to dissect me or are they Amazonian Woman who want to worship me as their love god?

WOMAN A. They are friendly, normal looking aliens and they want to give you eternal life in exchange for knowledge.

MAN B. What kind of knowledge?

WOMAN A. What do you mean, "What kind of knowledge?"

MAN B. Well, if they want to know about football, I'm all there, but I'm no Einstein. I mean, hey, if they can build a spaceship and fly to another planet, I doubt there's much I could teach them.

WOMAN A. Okay. We'll just say 'no' to that question. Question Number Three: If you could change one thing about yourself, what would it be?

MAN B. Do you mean my looks, personality, brains, my way with women, job skills...

WOMAN A. Anything. Whatever pops into your head.

MAN B. ...conversation, talent, family members, friends, taste in clothes...

WOMAN A. Any of those will do.

MAN B. The type of car I drive, favorite sports team, the beer I drink, whether I wear boxers or tighty whities...

WOMAN A. Anything! Is there something you don't like about yourself that you wish you could change?

MAN B. Oh boy, is there.

(*Pause.*)

WOMAN A. Well, what is it?

MAN B. You mean just one thing?

WOMAN A. Yes! Just one thing!

MAN B. Which thing?

WOMAN A. I don't know. I don't know you. Pick one.

MAN B. Well there's a lot of them.

WOMAN A. Listen, we're running out of time and we still have six questions to go.

MAN B. Five.

WOMAN A. Excuse me?

MAN B. Five. I already answered Number Four.

WOMAN A. Number Four?

MAN B. Brooklyn, remember?

WOMAN A. Number Four?

> (*gasping*)
>
> Four, yes.
>
> (*gasping*)
>
> Brooklyn.
>
> (*gasping*)
>
> You answered one.
>
> (*gasping*)
>
> You actually answered one question.
>
> (*gasping*)
>
> Help me.
>
> (*gasping*)
>
> Hyperventilating.

MAN B. Can I do anything for you?

> (*gasping*)

WOMAN A. Answer the questions.

> (*gasping*)
>
> Answer the questions.
>
> (*sobbing*)
>
> Answer...answer...answer...
>
> (*A bell rings.* **WOMAN A** *gets up and runs to the next chair sobbing. The two other women shift chairs.*)

MAN B. Wow! She was hot!

> (*Lights down on* **MAN B.** *Lights up on* **WOMAN C** *and* **MAN F.**)

MAN F. Hi.

WOMAN C. Hi.

MAN F. Listen, I know we're not supposed to give out any personal information, but I noticed you earlier and I'd like to get to know you. Here's my name and number.

(**MAN F** *checks to make sure no one is looking and then carefully hands* **WOMAN C** *a card.*)

WOMAN C. Thanks. I'd love to take your number. Here's mine.

(**WOMAN C** *checks to make sure no one is looking and then carefully hands* **MAN F** *a card.*)

MAN F. Thanks.

(*looking at the card*)

Nice name. It's my sister's name.

WOMAN C. Maybe it's an omen. Maybe we were meant to be together.

MAN F. Maybe.

WOMAN C. I couldn't help but notice you when I came in the room. You're really cute.

MAN F. Thanks. You are too.

WOMAN C. Thanks.

MAN F. So, is this your first time doing this?

WOMAN C. No. I've done it a few times.

MAN F. Oh yeah?

WOMAN C. Well, more than a few times. Several times. Actually, more then several times. Lots of times. In fact, I guess I've done it so much that you could call me an expert.

MAN F. Really?

WOMAN C. Really.

MAN F. So you must have some luck. I mean, meeting guys. I mean, dating guys from here.

WOMAN C. Sure. That's why I keep coming back. I've dated a lot of guys that I've met through here.

MAN F. A lot?

WOMAN C. Yeah.

MAN F. Anyone special?

WOMAN C. All of them. They were all special. Every last one of them.

MAN F. Really? All of them?

WOMAN C. Oh yes. Special guys like you.

MAN F. Like me?

WOMAN C. Uh huh.

MAN F. Um, thanks.

(*Pause.*)

So exactly how many of these special guys have you dated?

WOMAN C. I don't know. Twenty. Thirty, maybe.

MAN F. Twenty or thirty?

WOMAN C. Maybe more, I don't remember. I've been doing this for a while.

MAN F. I see.

WOMAN C. There are so many special people in the world.

MAN F. It sounds like you have a knack for finding them.

WOMAN C. That's what I've always thought, that I have this knack for finding special men.

MAN F. It's a real talent.

WOMAN C. But I guess I was wrong.

MAN B. Huh?

WOMAN C. If I was right then I wouldn't be back here all the time looking for that one special man, now would I?

MAN F. That's not true. You just haven't met the right one special man yet.

WOMAN C. But all those other men were so special and so dumped me. If I wasn't such a loser I would be with one of those special men right now.

MAN F. Oh come on...

WOMAN C. I would be in their arms, in their thoughts, in their dreams, in their beds.

MAN F. Okay.

(**MAN F** *starts to leave.*)

WOMAN C. I'm sorry. I just got carried away.

MAN F. Listen, I'm sure it wasn't your fault. Don't beat yourself up over it.

WOMAN C. You're so sweet and understanding. I can't believe how special you are.

MAN F. I'm not special. Not even close to being special.

WOMAN C. But you are. You're special.

(**MAN F** *struggles to get away.*)

MAN F. That's really sweet.

WOMAN C. I can't believe how lucky I am to have met you.

MAN F. I'm nobody special, really.

WOMAN C. But you are.

MAN F. I don't think so.

WOMAN C. And here I am with you.

MAN F. Well, you're not really with me. We're just talking.

WOMAN C. You gave me your number.

MAN F. Oh, yeah. About that...

WOMAN C. We're meant to be together.

MAN F. I'm not too sure about that.

WOMAN C. You're so special. I can't believe you don't have a girlfriend.

MAN F. Well, actually, I do.

WOMAN C. You do?

MAN F. Yeah. She's right over there.

(*He points to* **WOMAN A**)

We thought it would be fun to meet new people.

WOMAN C. Fun?

MAN F. Yeah. Hey, have you ever seen those reality shows where the couple gets put on an island with other couples and they have to try to keep their relationship together without cheating?

WOMAN C. Yeah.

MAN F. We tried it.

WOMAN C. Did you cheat?

MAN F. Sure. The studio won't pick you if don't wanna cheat.

WOMAN C. You cheated on your girlfriend and she's still with you?

MAN F. She cheated too.

WOMAN C. Wow!

MAN F. Yeah, wow-oh! Anything wrong?

WOMAN C. I was just thinking.

MAN F. About?

WOMAN C. How special you are.

MAN F. What?

WOMAN C. I've never met anyone as special as you.

MAN F. Oh great.

(*A bell rings.*)

Thank God!

(**WOMAN C** *stands to leave.*)

WOMAN C. Call me.

(**WOMAN C** *goes to another chair.*)

MAN F. What a wacko!

(*Lights down on* **MAN F.** *Lights up on* **WOMAN E** *and* **MAN D.**)

MAN D. Hi.

WOMAN E. Hi.

MAN D. Listen, I know we're not supposed to give out any personal information, but I noticed you earlier and I'd like to get to know you. Here's my name and number.

WOMAN E. Thanks, but maybe we shouldn't exchange numbers just yet.

MAN D. I'm sorry My friends told me to start like that. I shouldn't have listened.

WOMAN E. It's okay. So tell me about yourself. What do you do for a living?

MAN D. I'm a chef.

WOMAN E. Fun.

MAN D. I think so. I get to be creative, meet new people.

WOMAN E. Did you always want to cook?

MAN D. Oh yeah. My mom was a great cook. She used to make all these crazy dishes and I'd beg her to teach me how. She did.

WOMAN E. What about culinary school?

MAN D. I went to the Culinary Academy on Polk Street.

WOMAN E. No way! My best friend used to go there.

MAN D. What's her name or his name?

WOMAN E. Sharon Tate.

MAN D. I know Sharon. She makes this French chocolate crepe with plums that's mind-blowing.

WOMAN E. She made them for me last week.

MAN D. Did you ever come to the school?

WOMAN E. Once. These nuns were there.

MAN D. We have a special class for nuns.

WOMAN E. Really? They were all dressed in their habits and looked like a bunch of penguins. It reminded me of this old series called 'The Flying Nun.'

MAN D. Sally Field. I'd watch it sometimes before church.

WOMAN E. You're Catholic?

MAN D. Riordan High School, "Catholic excellence that reflects the cultural richness of the San Francisco Bay Area."

WOMAN E. Mercy High School, "A college preparatory for young Catholic women."

MAN D. When did you graduate?

WOMAN E. '01.

MAN D. Me too.

WOMAN E. Do you know James Jordan?

MAN D. He's my cousin.

WOMAN E. He was my prom date.

MAN D. Then you know Katie Foster?

WOMAN E. Of course.

MAN D. She was my best friend.

(*speaking together*)

WOMAN E. What a coincidence.

MAN D. What a coincidence.

(*speaking together*)

WOMAN E. So what...

MAN D. Do you...

WOMAN E. I'm sorry. Go ahead.

MAN D. Please, go ahead.

WOMAN E. You first.

MAN D. This is weird.

WOMAN E. Yeah, it is.

MAN D. So what do you do?

WOMAN E. I'm a writer.

MAN D. Cool. What kind of writing?

WOMAN E. I write for a magazine.

MAN D. Which one?

WOMAN E. California Food and Wine.

MAN D. You write for a food magazine?

WOMAN E. Uh huh. I write articles on famous chefs.

MAN D. You're kidding?

WOMAN E. No.

MAN D. Wow! This is crazy, all these coincidences.

WOMAN E. It is.

MAN D. We're both Catholic, graduated the same year, know the same people, like the same things, work in the same industry and show up at the same speed dating session.

WOMAN E. I like you.

MAN D. I like you too.

WOMAN E. I'd like to see you again.

MAN D. I'd like to see you again.

WOMAN E. Will you call me?

MAN D. I still have my name and number on that piece of paper.

(**MAN D** *takes the paper out of his pocket. As he hands her the paper, a* **GUARD** *rushes out of the wings and grabs the paper from his hand.*)

GUARD. What are doing?

(*looking at the paper*)

A name and a phone number. That's against the rules. You're disqualified. Leave.

MAN D. But we were...

GUARD. I don't care what you were doing. Rules are rules. The only exchange of information must come from me.

WOMAN E. Will you give him my number then?

GUARD. No. He broke the rules. He's disqualified. He has to leave.

WOMAN E. Then I'm leaving too.

GUARD. No you're not. You're not leaving this building until he's gone.

WOMAN E. But we're perfect for each other.

GUARD. You should have thought about that before breaking the rules.

(*To* **MAN D**)

Bye.

MAN D. But she's the one.

(**GUARD** *grabs* **MAN D** *by the arm and forces it behind his back in an arm lock.*)

GUARD. Listen lover boy, I've dealt with guys like you before. Out you go.

MAN D. But you can't take me away now.

WOMAN E. Please don't take him.

    (**GUARD** *is pushing* **MAN D** *off the stage.*)

MAN D. I'll find you.

WOMAN E. I'll find you.

MAN D. Come see me at work.

WOMAN E. You didn't tell me where you work.

MAN D. I work at...

    (**GUARD** *slaps his free hand over* **MAN D** *'s mouth. His voice is muffled.*)

GUARD. Ah, ah, ah.

    (**MAN D** *is drug off stage. Bell rings. Lights down.*)

PROPS

Notebook and pen
Bell

THE DRAG OF DATING

CHARACTERS

SCOTT
AARON
CONNER
JIMMY
VOICE

SETTING

Back stage in the dressing room of The Diamond
Mine, *the hottest female impersonator club in Chicago.
The room has a long dressing table with four chairs and
a few small, stand-alone mirrors. Makeup is strewn
across the table. A rack of flamboyant woman's clothing
is in the corner and a few pieces of clothing are thrown
over the chairs.*

(*The stage is dark.* **AARON** *enters and flips on the light switch. He throws a large shoulder bag he is carrying onto the floor next to a chair. He runs his hand through his hair, lets out a sigh, picks some clothes off of the rack, tosses them over the back of a chair, sits and begins to apply makeup to his face.* **SCOTT** *enters, puts down his things, goes to the clothes rack and looks through the clothes.*)

SCOTT. Airman. What's up?

AARON. Just another day in the Mine. How was your date last night?

SCOTT. Hot, but not.

AARON. Let me guess, sushi, a late night walk in the park which led to a snowball fight, a roll in the snow, a smoldering kiss and...

SCOTT. And a taxi ride home...alone.

AARON. Not even a kiss good night?

SCOTT. Oh yeah. She kissed me with her palm across my cheek when I tried to warm her up.

AARON. Ouch.

SCOTT. No worries. Tonight I'm seeing her friend Melissa.

AARON. You're a dog!

SCOTT. Better than being an old, married fart like you!

AARON. When you find the best, who needs to keep getting slapped.

SCOTT. You're cruel, Airman.

(**CONNER** *comes in, sets down his bag and goes to the clothes rack.*)

AARON. Hey Conner.

SCOTT. Conman, what's happening?

CONNER. Where's my blue dress?

SCOTT. The one with the sequins?

CONNER. No, the one with the poodle squares. Of course, the one with the sequins.

SCOTT. Josie took it.

CONNER. What?

SCOTT. She said it needed to be mended on one of the seams.

CONNER. That lying bitch! She knows that's my favorite dress!

AARON. She was just trying to help.

CONNER. She was trying to throw me off tonight.

AARON. You didn't see Carrie again last night, did you?

CONNER. Why is it that every time something happens between me and Josie everyone thinks I've been with Carrie?

SCOTT. Because it's true.

CONNER. We're just friends.

SCOTT. Uh huh.

AARON. Right.

CONNER. We are! I can't believe she took my blue dress. You know the press will be here tonight?

AARON. We know.

CONNER. The bitch!

SCOTT. Conner, why don't you just go and apologize? Maybe she'll give it back to you.

CONNER. That's what she wants. She wants me to grovel.

AARON. Then grovel, get your dress back and get ready.

SCOTT. If it was my favorite dress and the press was coming I'd grovel.

CONNER. You're right. What else can I do? I'll grovel.

AARON. Good luck.

(**CONNER** *exits.*)

AARON. Jimmy's late.

SCOTT. Again. Did he text you?

AARON. Uh uh.

SCOTT. That's not like him.

AARON. He probably just slept late.

(**JIMMY** *stumbles in. He's dirty, his clothes are torn and he falls to the ground.*)

Or not.

SCOTT. Jimster, you okay?

(**AARON** *gets up and feels* **JIMMY**'s *pulse.*)

AARON. He's not dead.

SCOTT. That's good. I'd hate to work double time tonight.

JIMMY. Thanks for the sympathies.

SCOTT. Yup, he's okay.

(**AARON** *drops* **JIMMY**'s *hand and goes back to putting on his makeup.*)

JIMMY. It's those damn groupies again. I can't get within three blocks of this place without getting mobbed.

SCOTT. Tough life.

JIMMY. You're jealous.

SCOTT. Why would I be jealous of a man who can't stop getting mobbed by every gay man in Chicago?

JIMMY. You forgot about all the hot babes too.

AARON. Can you two not start this again?

JIMMY. He started it.

SCOTT. You started it.

JIMMY. You're jealous.

(**CONNER** *enters carrying his blue dress.*)

CONNER. I'm just in time for the nightly catfight.

JIMMY. Kiss my girdle Conman.

CONNER. Nice to see you too, Jimmy. What's the fight about tonight? The fans, the mobs, the publicity calls, the wardrobe?

AARON. The mobs.

CONNER. Ah yes. It's hard to control the mobs.

JIMMY. You're all jealous.

AARON. You're right. Now get your makeup on. You're first tonight.

JIMMY. I can't be first. I'm in no condition to go on stage. Look at me. It'll take me at least an hour to do my hair. Scotty, switch with me?

SCOTT. Sorry loverboy. No way I'll be ready in time for first slot. The press is here tonight, you know.

JIMMY. Dear God, don't tell me that. It's not true? Say it's not true.

AARON. Press at eight.

JIMMY. Shit! My life is over. My career is over. I may as well just forget I ever lived.

AARON. I'll switch with you.

JIMMY. You will? You really will? Aaron, I love you.

AARON. Sorry, I'm taken.

(**JIMMY** *collapses into a chair.*)

JIMMY. At least I have a moment now to breathe.

(*A knock at the stage door.*)

VOICE. (*offstage*) Ten to press.

AARON. Thank you ten!

JIMMY. Hey, Scotty, how was your date last night?

SCOTT. Okay.

JIMMY. Did she slap you before or after the "let me warm you up" line?

SCOTT. Kiss my long eyelashes. I suppose you did better?

JIMMY. You remember the hot blond in the front row last night?

CONNER. You mean the one sitting next to Donald Trump?

AARON. Donald Trump was here?

CONNER. I'm talking about the guy with the bad toupee.

SCOTT. You mean the chick with the huge gazumbas?

JIMMY. That's her. She cooked me breakfast this morning.

SCOTT. You're lying.

(**JIMMY** *pulls out a very large bra from his bag.*)

JIMMY. She wanted me to wear it today, to remind me of last night.

SCOTT. You suck!

CONNER. Nice work Jimster.

AARON. Great color. Can I borrow it tomorrow? It matches the dress my wife bought me for our anniversary.

JIMMY. Only if you let me borrow the maroon boa.

AARON. Deal.

SCOTT. If I were bisexual I would get as many dates as you.

JIMMY. No chance.

CONNER. So what's Miss High Shelf's name?

JIMMY. Lola.

SCOTT. Lola? That's gotta be a fake name.

JIMMY. (*holding up the bra*) Wouldn't be the only thing she has that's fake.

AARON. I'm gonna go warm up. Play nicely, girls.

(**AARON** *exits through the door. Piano music plays and a woman's voice sings scales.*)

SCOTT. Airman sounds good tonight.

CONNER. Aaron sounds good every night. I wish I could have half his talent.

JIMMY. I wish I could have half his wife. Meow!

SCOTT. That was crass.

JIMMY. It was honest.

SCOTT. You'd sleep with anyone, wouldn't you?

JIMMY. I wouldn't sleep with you.

SCOTT. I should scratch your eyes out.

CONNER. Now girls!

(**AARON** *enters.*)

AARON. They just opened the doors and you're never gonna guess who's out there tonight.

JIMMY. The press?

AARON. Connor, you'd better see for yourself.

CONNER. Oh God, I don't like the sound of that.

(**CONNER** *rushes to the door, cracks it open a bit and peaks out. He slams the door and screams.*)

CONNER. Oh my God! It's Larissa Larue!

JIMMY. The nasty woman that gave you that horrid revue?

CONNER. Yes! Who invited her? Worse yet, who put her front and center?

SCOTT. Josie.

(*A knock.*)

AARON. Who is it?

VOICE. Flower delivery for Miss Mandy Malone.

CONNER. Flowers? For me?

(**CONNER** *opens the door and a bouquet of black roses is handed to him. He screams again.*)

Black roses! Somebody sent me black roses!

SCOTT. Is there a card?

(**CONNER** *pulls out a card and reads.*)

CONNER. "Good luck with the press tonight. I'm sure Ms. Larue will enjoy your performance just as much as she did the last time. Love, Josie."

AARON. She's really pissed this time.

CONNER. I can't believe she's doing this to me after all we've been through.

JIMMY. Yeah, after all you've put her through.

CONNER. This is not the time to be mean. I need sympathy.

SCOTT. You need more than that. You need a miracle.

CONNER. I just won't go on. Why humiliate myself?

AARON. She's just trying to psyche you out. Don't let her do that. Now put on your dress, go out there and show her that you're a better woman than she is.

CONNER. You're right.

(**CONNOR** *steps into the blue dress. He starts to pull it up and stops.*)

I can't do it.

AARON. Yes, you can.

(**AARON** *pulls up the dress. One side puckers. He struggles with it a moment, then realizes it's been altered.*)

Oh shit!

CONNER. My dress! My favorite dress! She's ruined it!

JIMMY. This is really bad! You're never gonna fix it.

CONNER. Thanks!

SCOTT. That's one cruel woman to do that to a man's favorite dress.

CONNER. What am I going to do?

AARON. Here.

(**AARON** *reaches into his bag and pulls out a beautiful evening gown.*)

My an anniversary present. You can wear it tonight.

JIMMY. It does go great with the bra. Here.

(**JIMMY** *hands* **CONNER** *the bra.*)

SCOTT. These shoes will look fabulous on you.

(**SCOTT** *hands shoes to* **CONNER.**)

CONNER. I don't know what to say. You're the best friends a girl could ever have.

AARON. Let's get you together.

(*They dress* **CONNER.**)

CONNER. I want to say one thing. Carrie and I are just friends.

SCOTT. We know.

JIMMY. And we also know that Josie's a nut case.

AARON. But how you gonna tell your friend his girlfriend's a psycho?

CONNER. Guess I had to learn the hard way.

SCOTT. Sometimes dating can be a real drag.

JIMMY. Literally, darling.

(*offstage*)

VOICE. And now ladies and gentlemen. The Gold Mine is proud to present an evening with some of the most talented and beautiful ladies in Chicago.

SCOTT. Here we go. Break legs, everyone!

(**AARON, SCOTT** *and* **JIMMY** *continue to beautify* **CONNER.**)

VOICE. We have an amazing line-up for you tonight. Our first lovely lady has the voice of an angel and the face of dream.

SCOTT. There! You're beautiful!

AARON. Wow! You look better in that dress than I do!

CONNER. You think so?

JIMMY. What are you doing after the show gorgeous?

CONNER. Jimmy, you would date me?

JIMMY. Yeah, if I didn't know you.

(**CONNER** *kisses* **JIMMY** *on the cheek.*)

CONNER. Thank you all so much.

VOICE. She hails from Vancouver, British Columbia.

AARON. What?

VOICE. Our own goddess from the north, Miss Mandy Malone.

CONNER. Me?

AARON. I was supposed to be first.

JIMMY. Josie.

SCOTT. Conner, can you do it?

CONNER. Look at me. I'm fabulous. I'll show Miss Psycho who's the boss. Out of my way ladies. I'm coming out. Well, not like that, but you know what I mean.

(**CONNER** *exits. Audience applause is heard. A piano plays a sexy song.*)

SCOTT. That's not his usual song.

AARON. It's a statement from Josie.

JIMMY. Don't worry about him. I happen to know it's one of his favorite songs.

(AARON, SCOTT *and* JIMMY *peak out the stage door.*)

SCOTT. He's amazing.

AARON. I've never heard him sing so well.

JIMMY. I've never seen him dance so well.

SCOTT. Look at what he's doing to Ms. Larue.

AARON. She's eating out of the palm of his hand.

JIMMY. He's so sexy.

AARON. Don't even think about it.

JIMMY. I can think about it, I just can't do anything about it.

SCOTT. He has them mesmerized.

(*The music stops and the audience claps wildly.* CONNER *comes through the door out of breath with a bouquet of flowers.*)

CONNER. Did you see me? Did you see me? I was good.

SCOTT. Good is not the word for it. Amazing!

AARON. Spectacular, incredible.

JIMMY. Hot, scaldingly sexy.

CONNER. Down boy!

JIMMY. Sorry.

CONNER. I feel like a new woman. I couldn't have done it without you. All of you. Thank you so much.

(*A knock at the door.* SCOTT *opens it and is handed a note.*)

SCOTT. It's for you.

(*He hands the note to* CONNER.)

CONNER. I wonder who it's from.

AARON. Why don't you open it?

(**CONNER** *opens the note and reads. He gasps.*)

SCOTT. Well, Conman. What does it say?

CONNER. You're a hot, sexy beast. Meow! Your number one fan. Larissa Larue.

(**CONNER** *screams. A knock on the door.* **SCOTT** *opens it and is handed a note.*)

SCOTT. Another one for you.

JIMMY. I'm getting jealous.

SCOTT. Hah!

(**CONNER** *opens the note and reads.*)

AARON. Well?

CONNER. It's from Jerry.

SCOTT. The owner? I didn't know he was here tonight.

AARON. Josie probably invited him thinking that Conner was gonna bomb.

JIMMY. That beeatch!

AARON. What does it say?

CONNER. Dear Ms. Malone. I'm aware of the sabotage Ms. Jasper caused for you this evening and, at great risk to myself, I have terminated her employment. Please accept my sincerest gratitude for an incredible performance produced against all odds. You are a true professional. Kindest regards, Jerry Bascom.

SCOTT. He fired Josie.

AARON. Hope he has some good body guards.

JIMMY. He'll have to use the secret tunnel to leave tonight.

(**CONNER** *cries.*)

SCOTT. Conman, you okay?

CONNER. I can't believe it.

JIMMY. That Josie was fired?

CONNER. This whole evening. It's been something else.

JIMMY. You can say that again.

CONNER. It's changed my life.

AARON. What do you mean?

CONNER. When I walked in here tonight, I just wanted to die. Now look at me.

JIMMY. You're fabulous, darling.

AARON. Why did you want to die?

CONNER. I lost my confidence. That's why I've been seeing Carrie. She's my therapist.

SCOTT. You didn't tell us.

CONNER. I didn't think you cared. I thought I was just another pretty face.

AARON. You're our friend.

JIMMY. You're one of us.

SCOTT. And we're a rare breed. Gotta stick together.

CONNER. You showed me that tonight. Giving me the clothes, helping me with my hair. Scott, these shoes are dynamite. Can I keep them?

SCOTT. Sorry sister.

CONNER. It doesn't matter anyway. Look at me. I've never looked this good in my life and it's all because of you. My friends.

JIMMY. Group hug.

(*They hug.* JIMMY *grabs* CONNER*'s butt. A knock at the door.*)

(*Offstage*)

VOICE. Ms. Baxter, you're on in two.

AARON. Thank you two.

JIMMY. Hey, Conner, how'd you like to go out for a drink after the show? You know, just a couple of buddies having a beer.

CONNER. Sorry, I can't. I need to see my therapist.

SCOTT. I thought you were all good now?

CONNER. I am.

SCOTT. Then why are you seeing Carrie?

CONNER. To thank her for her help, to ask her on a date

and to tell her that I got hit on by the hottest guy in Chicago and turned him down cold! I'm hot! Oh yeah! Who's hot? I'm hot!

(**CONNER** *dances to the rack and starts to change.*)

SCOTT. Well Jimster. Guess the options are a little slimmer than you thought, eh?

JIMMY. I was just trying to make him feel good. I already have a date tonight with Larissa Larue.

SCOTT. What?

JIMMY. Shhh! I knew she was coming and didn't think Conner could pull it off on his own, so I gave her a little incentive.

SCOTT. That was a nice thing to do. I didn't know you had it in you.

JIMMY. Yeah, well don't say anything, okay?

(*offstage*)

VOICE. Ms. Baxter, you're on.

AARON. Wish me luck!

CONNER. You don't need any luck, honey. I got 'em all warmed up for you.

(**AARON** *exits. Lights down.*)

PROPS

Make up
Wigs
Ladies evening gowns
Clothes rack
Table top mirrors
Ladies shoes

THE DATING GAME

CHARACTERS

LUCY

ANNOUNCER

CHUCK

BACHELOR NUMBER ONE

BACHELOR NUMBER TWO

BACHELOR NUMBER THREE.

SETTING

A dating service formatted after the game show "The Dating Game." One chair is center stage. A wall separates three other chairs from the solitary chair.

(**LUCY** *wanders onto stage.*)

LUCY. Hello? Is anyone here? I'm not sure I'm in the right place. I'm looking for a dating service.

ANNOUNCER (V.O.). You've come to the right place. And now, your host Chuck Ferret.

(**CHUCK FERRET** *runs onto stage, through the audience kissing people on the cheek and blowing kisses.*)

CHUCK. Thank you. Thank you. Thank you. It's lovely to see you all here again today.

(*Handing a card to a woman in the audience.*)

Hey. How ya doin' beautiful? Why don't you ditch this loser and call me later?

LUCY. Excuse me. Is this a dating service?

ANNOUNCER (V.O.). Welcome to The Dating Game. Tonight we have three eager bachelors waiting to take you on the date of your dreams.

LUCY. Who said that?

ANNOUNCER (V.O.). The Announcer.

LUCY. Okay.

CHUCK. And tonight's contestant comes to us from?

LUCY. I was just walking by.

CHUCK. Out on the street. She is a lovely girl whose hobbies are?

LUCY. Hobbies?

CHUCK. She's cute and her hobbies are?

LUCY. Swimming, tennis and zorbing.

CHUCK. Zorbing? What's zorbing?

LUCY. It's rolling around in a large dual paneled acrylic ball in a grassy field like a hamster.

CHUCK. There you go studio audience. And now, the name of tonight's contestant is?

LUCY. Lucy.

CHUCK. Let's hear a big round of applause for Lucy.

LUCY. I don't think I'm in the right place.

CHUCK. Sure you are, Lucy. Come on over here and have a seat. It's time to meet your three bachelors. Bachelor Number One hails from the Midwest. His interests are snowshoeing, kite flying and gourmet cooking. Let's give a nice round of applause for Bachelor Number One.

(**BACHELOR NUMBER ONE** *enters.*)

BACHELOR NUMBER ONE. Hey Lucy, let me fly you to the moon on one of my kites.

LUCY. Oh, that was nice.

BACHELOR NUMBER ONE. Thanks.

CHUCK. Bachelor Number Two is an actor, a body builder and the brother of Jonny Depp. Say hello to Bachelor Number Two.

(**BACHELOR NUMBER TWO** *enters blowing kisses to the crowd.*)

BACHELOR NUMBER TWO. Hey Lucy. What's happenin'?

LUCY. I didn't know Jonny Depp had a brother.

CHUCK. He doesn't, but it's great for the ratings. Bachelor Number Three loves hiking, biking, surfing and watching Hawaiian sunsets. He also has a collection of original Warner Brothers artwork. Put your hands together for Bachelor Number Three.

(**BACHELOR NUMBER THREE** *enters and gives a Hawaiian hand motion.*)

BACHELOR NUMBER THREE. Aloha Lucy.

LUCY. Hi Bachelor Number Three.

CHUCK. Have a seat bachelors. Lucy, all of your bachelors are now in place. Are you ready with your questions?

LUCY. Questions?

CHUCK. Don't worry your pretty little head. The network has paid writers to make sure we have questions that will be interesting and keep the audience happy. Here you go.

(**CHUCK** *pulls index cards from his pocket and hands them to* **LUCY**.)

LUCY. Thank you.

(**LUCY** *looks through the questions.*)

CHUCK. Don't get them out of order.

LUCY. I didn't know they were in any order.

CHUCK. They are so don't mix them up. Well, it looks like we're ready to go. Take it away Lucy.

LUCY. Okay.

(*reading*)

Um, Bachelor Number Two. If you were a flower, what kind of flower would you be?

BACHELOR NUMBER TWO. I'd be a Venus fly trap and trap you in my fly Venus.

LUCY. Did the writers write that?

BACHELOR NUMBER TWO. Yup.

LUCY. Okay. Bachelor Number Three, same question.

BACHELOR NUMBER THREE. I would be a lei of orchids to adorn your beautiful neck.

LUCY. That was a nice answer.

BACHELOR NUMBER THREE. It was all mine, Lucy.

LUCY. Original? I'm impressed.

BACHELOR NUMBER ONE. What about me? Wanna know what kind of flower I'd be?

CHUCK. Bachelor Number One, please don't address the contestant unless she addresses you.

BACHELOR NUMBER ONE. But I have a good answer for that question.

CHUCK. Lucy, stick with the cards and ignore the man behind the wall.

LUCY. Sorry Bachelor Number One.

(*reading*)

Bachelor Number Three, you're driving down the road

and late for work when you see a horrible accident. What do you do?

BACHELOR NUMBER THREE. I'd pull over, call 911 and check to see if there's anything I can do to help the injured victims.

LUCY. What about your job?

BACHELOR NUMBER THREE. It would be wrong to abandon people in need. My boss should understand that.

LUCY. That's very noble of you.

BACHELOR NUMBER THREE. Thank you.

LUCY. You're welcome. Bachelor Number Two. If you could be any actor who would it be and why?

BACHELOR NUMBER TWO. Hey, my brother Jonny cause he's the greatest.

LUCY. Yes he is. How cool is it to have Jonny Depp as your brother?

BACHELOR NUMBER TWO. It's pretty cool.

LUCY. I bet.

BACHELOR NUMBER ONE. Can we get on with this?

CHUCK. This is your second warning Bachelor Number One.

BACHELOR NUMBER ONE. I'm getting bored over here.

CHUCK. Why don't you plug in your iPod? Go ahead Lucy.

LUCY. All right Chuck. Bachelor Number Three. If you were the Coyote chasing the Road Runner, how would you catch him?

BACHELOR NUMBER THREE. I don't believe in cruelty to animals so the only reason I'd be chasing him if I was going to invite him to come to my house for dinner and for that I'd probably send him an eVite.

LUCY. That is so sweet. Thank you Bachelor Number Three. Bachelor Number Two...

BACHELOR NUMBER ONE. Hey, what about me? Don't I get any questions?

CHUCK. How many times do I have to tell you?

(**CHUCK** *walks around the wall to* **BACHELOR NUMBER ONE**.)

Stick with the script. If you keep interrupting we'll never get finished.

BACHELOR NUMBER ONE. But I'm not doing anything over here.

CHUCK. She'll get around to you sooner or later. Wait your turn.

BACHELOR NUMBER ONE. Easy for you to say. You're doing something.

CHUCK. Of course I'm doing something. I'm the host. Now be quiet!

(**CHUCK** *walks back to* **LUCY**.)

Go ahead Lucy.

LUCY. Bachelor Number Two. If there was one thing you could change about Bachelor Number One, what would it be?

BACHELOR NUMBER TWO. It's a toss up between his looks and his attitude.

BACHELOR NUMBER THREE. That's two things.

CHUCK. I'd change his attitude.

BACHELOR NUMBER ONE. Hey! Why am I being picked on here? All I wanted to do was come on the show, have some fun and maybe get a date with a nice girl.

CHUCK. That's all? Well, you gotta work for it buddy!

LUCY. You're right Bachelor Number One.

CHUCK. Lucy, you can't talk to him. You have to follow the format.

LUCY. I'm the client. I can talk to them any way I want.

CHUCK. But that's not how the show works.

LUCY. I didn't come here to be on a show. I came to find a nice guy to go on a date with.

BACHELOR NUMBER ONE. You tell him Lucy.

CHUCK. Bachelor Number One, if I have to tell you one more time...

LUCY. Shut up Chuck. I'm the star of this show and I'm taking over. It's time to start doing things my way.

(*She tosses the index cards up in the air*)

Bachelors, are you in?

BACHELOR NUMBER ONE. I'm with you, girl.

BACHELOR NUMBER THREE. Me too.

BACHELOR NUMBER TWO. I was supposed to win.

LUCY. You'll just have to take your chances like the other guys.

BACHELOR NUMBER TWO. But I'm not good at improv.

LUCY. Then leave now or stay and try to win.

BACHELOR NUMBER TWO. I took the day off from the car wash. I might as well stay.

LUCY. Great.

(*she sits*)

Now, Bachelor Number One.

CHUCK. But...

LUCY. Shh! Don't go there Chuck. Be a good boy and have a seat.

(**CHUCK** *sits.*)

Bachelor Number One. Tell me your idea of the perfect date.

BACHELOR NUMBER ONE. You and me on a snowmobile, wind blowing through our hair, you holding on tight around my waist.

LUCY. Can I drive?

BACHELOR NUMBER ONE. Me holding on tight around your waist.

LUCY. Perfect.

BACHELOR NUMBER ONE. We cruise to a cabin in a snow covered field, start a fire, drink wine and talk 'till the sun comes up.

LUCY. Now that's what I'm talking about. Can either of you other bachelors top that?

BACHELOR NUMBER THREE. I can. We would hike through a Hawaiian rain forest, find all the waterfalls and swim naked in their pools. Afterwards, we would rest on the beach, drinking Pina Coladas and watching the sunset.

LUCY. Ooh, that sounds nice too. Bachelor Number Two?

BACHELOR NUMBER TWO. We could call my brother and see if we could borrow his jet and fly to Europe.

LUCY. Jonny Depp isn't really your brother.

BACHELOR NUMBER TWO. Well, I know this three dollar theatre downtown that makes pretty good popcorn.

LUCY. I like popcorn. What movie would we see?

BACHELOR NUMBER TWO. Whatever we haven't seen yet. God, that was a stupid answer. Why couldn't you stick with the script?

LUCY. Because the script is nothing but lies.

BACHELOR NUMBER TWO. But I'm an actor. Give me a script and I'll be whatever you want me to be.

LUCY. Be yourself Bachelor Number Two. That's what I want.

CHUCK. That may not be a good idea.

LUCY. Why? Is he an ax murderer or something?

CHUCK. He'd be a lot more interesting if he was.

BACHELOR NUMBER TWO. Don't push me Chuck.

CHUCK. Yeah, whatever.

LUCY. Look Chuck, I'm not sure you understand what dating's all about. It's about accepting people for who they are and finding someone who compliments who you are.

CHUCK. Well, right now I'm really confused.

LUCY. I don't think that's anything new. Why don't you just have a seat and I'll handle this.

CHUCK. Um, Lucy, excuse me. I need a station break.

LUCY. Go ahead. We can do without you for a little while.

CHUCK. Thanks.

(**CHUCK** *exits.*)

LUCY. Talk to me Bachelor Number Two.

BACHELOR NUMBER TWO. This was supposed to be an easy job.

LUCY. Relax and be yourself.

BACHELOR NUMBER TWO. You won't like myself. I'm an actor who works at a car wash as my day job. My parents wanted me to be a doctor. Imagine how disappointed they are.

LUCY. Are you disappointed?

BACHELOR NUMBER TWO. No way. I love being an actor. It's the greatest job in the world and even though there's humiliating moments like now, I wouldn't do anything else.

LUCY. You sound pretty wonderful to me.

BACHELOR NUMBER TWO. Yeah?

LUCY. Yeah. How about you Bachelor Number Three?

BACHELOR NUMBER ONE. Here we go again.

BACHELOR NUMBER THREE. Dude, relax. The lady's workin' here. She's a nice girl. She's not gonna blow you off. Just hang loose.

BACHELOR NUMBER ONE. Sorry. I'll just be quiet and wait my turn.

BACHELOR NUMBER THREE. I'm a surfing pro.

LUCY. Cool.

BACHELOR NUMBER THREE. But I'm afraid of sharks.

LUCY. Lots of people are afraid of sharks.

BACHELOR NUMBER THREE. Yeah, but you can't surf if you're afraid of being in the ocean.

LUCY. Were you always afraid of sharks?

BACHELOR NUMBER THREE. No, my friend got bit a few months back and I haven't been able to go in the water since.

LUCY. Maybe you could talk to your friend and the two of you could help each other.

BACHELOR NUMBER THREE. You mean like a support group?

LUCY. Exactly.

BACHELOR NUMBER THREE. Good idea, Lucy. Thanks.

LUCY. You're welcome. Bachelor Number One, are you still there?

BACHELOR NUMBER ONE. I'm here, Lucy.

LUCY. Tell me about you.

BACHELOR NUMBER ONE. First of all, I'm not good at waiting my turn.

BACHELOR NUMBER TWO. We noticed.

BACHELOR NUMBER ONE. But I am good at knowing when to listen.

BACHELOR NUMBER TWO. I'll be quiet.

LUCY. What do you do Bachelor Number One?

BACHELOR NUMBER ONE. I own a little kite shop just outside of Chicago. I've loved kites since I was a kid. My sister and I would make kites out of anything we could find - newspapers, pillow cases, Dad's old shirts, car parts. I can pretty much make a kite out of anything.

BACHELOR NUMBER TWO. How about an anchor?

BACHELOR NUMBER ONE. Okay. Almost anything.

BACHELOR NUMBER TWO. I'll be quiet.

BACHELOR NUMBER ONE. I just feel lucky that I can do something I love every day.

BACHELOR NUMBER TWO. I know what you mean. Acting is my life. I can't imagine a day without it.

BACHELOR NUMBER THREE. Mohala i ka wai ka maka o ka pua.

LUCY. That's beautiful. What does it mean?

BACHELOR NUMBER THREE. Unfolded by the water are the faces of the flowers. Flowers thrive where there is water, as thriving people are found where life is good.

LUCY. In other words, do what you love and you'll be happy.

BACHELOR NUMBER THREE. You're a smart flower.

(**CHUCK** *enters.*)

CHUCK. Lucy, I hate to cut this short, but it's time for us to go to a commercial.

LUCY. Chuck, this isn't a TV show, it's a dating service. There are no cameras and no sponsors.

ANNOUNCER (V.O.). There's an Announcer.

LUCY. You're kinda creepy.

ANNOUNCER (V.O.). Just doing my job.

CHUCK. Okay, so we're not on TV, but we have to stick to the format. If we don't have a commercial then you don't have the time to think about your choice.

LUCY. I don't need time to think about my choice.

CHUCK. Then let's get this over with. It's been a rough day for me. Lucy, it's a tough decision, but you can only choose one man to be your date.

LUCY. Why do I only have to choose one?

CHUCK. Didn't you read the contract?

LUCY. I never got a contract.

CHUCK. It outlines your residual payments for syndication as well as photo rights to any children that may result from the selected bachelor.

LUCY. You're nuts.

CHUCK. Why does everyone say that to me after we discuss the contract?

LUCY. I thought that before you mentioned the contract.

CHUCK. Lucy, we need your decision. The Newlywed Game needs this space.

LUCY. All right all ready. First I want to say thanks, Chuck. These guys are great. It's a tough choice.

CHUCK. Yeah, yeah, yeah. Can you just make your choice and get this over with?

LUCY. Okay bachelors. I think that you're all great guys and I'd like to get to know each of you better. What would you think about leaving and getting a pizza?

CHUCK. All of you?

LUCY. Yes. All of us.

CHUCK. You can't take all three guys.

BACHELOR NUMBER ONE. I'm hungry. Let's go.

(**BACHELOR NUMBER ONE** *gets up and comes around the corner. He hugs* **LUCY.**)

LUCY. Bachelor Number One?

BACHELOR NUMBER ONE. That's right.

LUCY. Thanks for being patient.

BACHELOR NUMBER ONE. No worries. It was worth it.

CHUCK. What are you doing?

LUCY. Bachelor Number Two?

BACHELOR NUMBER TWO. I can't believe I didn't lose!

(**BACHELOR NUMBER TWO** *gets up and runs around the wall to* **LUCY.** *He hugs her.*)

LUCY. Bachelor Number Two?

BACHELOR NUMBER TWO. Yeah. I didn't lose. Sweet!

CHUCK. Stop this! You can't do this!

LUCY. Bachelor Number Three?

BACHELOR NUMBER THREE. Hawaiian pizza is my favorite.

(**BACHELOR NUMBER THREE** *comes around the corner and hugs* **LUCY.**)

LUCY. Bachelor Number Three.

BACHELOR NUMBER THREE. Aloha Lucy. You're a wise woman.

LUCY. Who's ready for pizza? My treat.

BACHELOR NUMBER ONE. We'll go dutch.

BACHELOR NUMBER TWO. I thought we were having pizza.

BACHELOR NUMBER ONE. We are. Never mind.

(*The* **BACHELORS** *and* **LUCY** *start to leave.*)

CHUCK. But you can't just leave like this.

LUCY. Why not?

CHUCK. You have to pick only one.

LUCY. I'd rather walk out with three friends then one date. Hey, why don't you come too. And bring the Announcer.

ANNOUNCER (V.O.). Thanks Lucy.

LUCY. No problem.

CHUCK. Can I order the pizza?

ANNOUNCER (V.O.). That's my job, Chuck.

CHUCK. I'm not getting to do anything today.

BACHELOR NUMBER ONE. Be patient. You'll get to do something sometime.

CHUCK. I know what I can do. Can I at least lead everyone in the farewell kiss?

LUCY. That would be awesome!

(*Everyone on stage pulls back with their hands to their mouths and blows a kiss to the audience the same way they used to do on The Dating Game.*)

CHUCK. Good night and good luck in love!

(*Theme music plays. Lights out.*)

PROPS

Microphone

THE ABC'S OF DATING

CHARACTERS

LIBBY

CAROLINA

TATI

SETTING

The play can be set anyplace which girls meet after school, a park or perhaps the bedroom of one of the girls.

(**LIBBY, CAROLINA** *and* **TATI** *each have a notebook.*)

LIBBY. Alexander.

CAROLINA. Anthony.

TATI. Aaron.

CAROLINA. Check.

LIBBY. Brett.

CAROLINA. Brian.

TATI. Bruce.

CAROLINA. Done.

LIBBY. Christopher.

CAROLINA. He was cute.

TATI. Can I call him?

LIBBY. That would defeat the whole purpose of the club.

TATI. But he was so cute. Can't we make an exception?

LIBBY. No.

TATI. But...

LIBBY. If you don't want to be a part of the club anymore, that's fine. Betray us for a boy. Go ahead.

TATI. Never!

LIBBY. Good.

TATI. But he was really cute.

LIBBY. Where was I?

CAROLINA. C's.

LIBBY. Christopher.

CAROLINA. Calum.

TATI. Cody.

CAROLINA. That's the C's.

LIBBY. Let's see. Daniel.

CAROLINA. Danger.

TATI. Danger doesn't count. That's not his real name.

LIBBY. What is his real name?

CAROLINA. Charlie.

TATI. Then you double did the C's.

CAROLINA. But his Mom calls him by his middle name.

LIBBY. Which is?

CAROLINA. Dartagnan.

TATI. Like the Musketeer?

CAROLINA. Don't laugh. He hates it.

LIBBY. I'm calling him Dart from now on.

CAROLINA. Don't do that. He'll know I told.

TATI. Or maybe Mouseketeer.

CAROLINA. Guys, please don't.

LIBBY. We won't. We're just kidding.

TATI. Speak for yourself.

CAROLINA. Tati.

TATI. All right.

LIBBY. We'll count him as a D. Dartagnan. Tati?

TATI. How about Dex? Does he count?

CAROLINA. He's your brother.

TATI. I couldn't get a D to go to the dance with me so he went.

CAROLINA. That's pathetic.

TATI. Like Dartagnan is any better?

CAROLINA. His name is Danger.

LIBBY. No, his name is Charlie. Let's just put a question mark next to the D's and if another D comes along you can both make up the letter. Fair?

CAROLINA. Fair.

TATI. Fair.

LIBBY. All right. E's. Edmund.

TATI. And Edan.

CAROLINA. Who?

TATI. The guys at the video store.

CAROLINA. What guys?

LIBBY. Oh, you were sick that day.

CAROLINA. You went through the E's without me?

TATI. It wasn't like we planned on meeting them.

CAROLINA. You both got E's in one day while I was dying in bed?

TATI. You had allergies.

CAROLINA. To a bee sting. It was traumatic.

LIBBY. You can do the E's later.

CAROLINA. I feel so left out.

TATI. Sorry.

CAROLINA. I'll take an exchange.

LIBBY. What do you want?

CAROLINA. Christopher.

TATI. That's not fair. Just because she had a runny nose she gets to call Christopher. What would I get for pneumonia?

CAROLINA. A nurse named Hildegard at the local hospital.

TATI. Very funny.

LIBBY. All right. We'll just do the E's over, together.

CAROLINA. But that means you get two E's.

TATI. We could start at the beginning again.

CAROLINA. Yeah, let's start again.

LIBBY. But we've only made our way through the first part of the alphabet. The deal was that we go all the way through the alphabet before we start over.

CAROLINA. How many guys do you think have a name that starts with the letter X?

TATI. It depends on what country you're in.

CAROLINA. California.

LIBBY. That's not a country.

CAROLINA. No, but we're in it! How many guys in California do you think have a name that begins with X?

TATI. She's right. We'll never make it through the whole alphabet.

LIBBY. We can put a time limit on the harder letters, like two weeks for Q. If no Q shows up, we move on.

CAROLINA. Two weeks? I can't go two weeks without dating a boy. Let's make it two days instead.

TATI. How about a compromise? One boy per letter per week. Whoever finishes the alphabet first wins.

LIBBY. That sounds like fun.

CAROLINA. Are we starting over?

TATI. Yes. And no using boys we've already dated.

LIBBY. No!

CAROLINA. But I want to date Christopher.

TATI. Maybe we could each pick one boy to see again?

LIBBY. What?

TATI. I wouldn't mind seeing Edan again.

LIBBY. You can't do that! The club rules say you can only see each boy once. How are you going to get through the alphabet if you keep repeating letters?

TATI. I'm young. I've got time.

CAROLINA. Maybe we're too mature to be in a club like this.

LIBBY. What do you mean?

CAROLINA. Well, maybe we should just date one boy, not a whole bunch.

LIBBY. Wait! What's going on here? We are the girls that formed the A to Z Club. We haven't even gotten through the L's yet and you're already into serious relationships?

CAROLINA. You said yourself that Chris is hot.

LIBBY. That's not the point. We started this club to promote diversity in dating. Too many of our peers are getting tied down in relationships before they've really had a chance to explore the vast expanse of boys in the world. And now the two of you are going against the entire purpose of this club. I wanna puke.

TATI. You're right. No boy is worth breaking our oath. Edan and I can be friends.

CAROLINA. And I guess I can be friends with Chris.

LIBBY. That's better. Remember the credo: Diversity in dating breeds knowledge, not marriage.

CAROLINA. No marriage before thirty.

TATI. No marriage before thirty.

LIBBY. Good. Now let's get back to work. What letter are we on?

CAROLINA. F.

LIBBY. Forrest.

CAROLINA. Freddie.

TATI. Frey.

CAROLINA. Shut up!

TATI. What?

CAROLINA. You did not go out with Frey!

TATI. We went to paint ball last weekend.

LIBBY. I am so jealous.

TATI. So there is someone you want to go out with.

LIBBY. I didn't say that.

CAROLINA. You didn't have to.

LIBBY. Did you kiss him?

TATI. At paint ball?

CAROLINA. Oh, come on. We know you.

TATI. It was just a little kiss.

LIBBY. Now I'm really jealous.

TATI. It was nothing. We're just friends.

CAROLINA. Isn't he a model for Mervyn's or someplace like that?

TATI. Gap.

LIBBY. He is so cute.

TATI. Can we just move on to the G's?

CAROLINA. No. I want details.

LIBBY. Me too.

TATI. Details of what? The color of paint we used?

CAROLINA. You know what we want.

TATI. I don't kiss and tell.

LIBBY. We'd do it for you.

CAROLINA. We've done it for you!

TATI. G. Garrett.

LIBBY. You went out with his brother too?

CAROLINA. Hussy!

TATI. You're just jealous!

CAROLINA. I can't believe you went out with both of them!

LIBBY. Now that's what I call diversity.

CAROLINA. I'm so jealous I could burn!

LIBBY. Well, we know who's in the lead so far.

CAROLINA. No! We said quantity, not quality. Besides, one date with her brother cancels out two dates with the hot guys.

TATI. There's no cancelling of anything. I earned the F and G.

LIBBY. You did, with two hot guys and we hate you for it.

TATI. You do?

LIBBY. No, we just want to be you. Frey and Garrett. I would give anything.

CAROLINA. Lucky girl. G.

LIBBY. Gary.

CAROLINA. You've had a crush on him ever since fifth grade.

LIBBY. He's sweet.

CAROLINA. And cute.

TATI. With nice eyes.

CAROLINA. Nice everything.

LIBBY. Yeah.

TATI. My mom thinks you two are going to get married.

LIBBY. That's silly.

CAROLINA. Why?

LIBBY. We're best friends.

TATI. Uh huh.

LIBBY. We are.

TATI. I mean 'uh huh' as in that's even more reason to think you two will get married.

LIBBY. Why would that mean anything?

CAROLINA. You spend more time with him than you do with us.

LIBBY. That's not true.

TATI. Let's see your cell phone.

LIBBY. Why?

TATI. How many text messages do you have from him today?

LIBBY. I don't know.

TATI. Five? Seven? A hundred?

LIBBY. What does it matter?

CAROLINA. And when's the last time you went with his family somewhere?

LIBBY. You know we went to visit his grandma last weekend.

TATI. Case closed.

LIBBY. Listen, Gary and I are just friends and no one, whether it's you two or your mother, are going to make it into anything more.

CAROLINA. Okay. Where were we? Oh yes, Gary, I mean, G. Gerald.

TATI. From the library Gerald?

CAROLINA. Yes. He's very studious.

LIBBY. Don't ever say anything again about Tati dating her brother.

TATI. It wasn't a date. It was a utility.

LIBBY. I'd go out with Tati's brother over Gerald any day.

CAROLINA. No way. Gerald is very enlightening.

LIBBY. Not exactly the first word that comes to my mind.

TATI. More like scrawny, greasy-haired, dweeb.

CAROLINA. Okay, I was having some trouble with science and he helped me out. Isn't that what damsels in distress are supposed to do?

LIBBY. Usually they look for a knight in shining armor, not a shiny knight with Armor All.

TATI. Was he any good at tutoring?

CAROLINA. I got a B on my test.

LIBBY. It was worth it then. Are we done with the G's?

CAROLINA. Yes. H?

LIBBY. Hank.

TATI. He's cool.

CAROLINA. Hagen.

LIBBY. Isn't he the new guy?

CAROLINA. Yes.

TATI. He's got an accent. Is he from the Midwest?

CAROLINA. Germany.

TATI. That's right. I went out with Heath.

LIBBY. Let me guess.

CAROLINA. Skateboarding.

LIBBY. Skateboarding.

TATI. Of course.

CAROLINA. Was he a good kisser?

TATI. Not as good as Garrett.

CAROLINA. You kissed Garrett and Frey?

TATI. Frey's kiss didn't count. It was just a victory kiss at paintball because I tagged a guy.

LIBBY. And Garrett's kiss?

TATI. That was real.

CAROLINA. We hate you, you know that?

TATI. You should. It was amazing!

LIBBY. Okay, anybody have an I?

CAROLINA. I went out went John and Ian.

TATI. The twins?

CAROLINA. Yeah.

LIBBY. You went out with both of them at the same time?

CAROLINA. They never go anywhere without each other. They should have been Siamese twins.

TATI. That could have been fun.

LIBBY. What did the three of you do on your date?

TATI. Does it matter?

CAROLINA. Avoiding the question? Now we have to know.

TATI. It was stupid.

LIBBY. Do tell.

TATI. They showed me how to make bombs with water bottles and dry ice.

LIBBY. You have the most interesting dates.

TATI. They're totally juvenile.

CAROLINA. But how do they kiss?

TATI. I didn't kiss them.

CAROLINA. Sure.

TATI. Okay Miss Critic, who was your I?

CAROLINA. I asked out Isaac, but he's still going out with Katie.

LIBBY. They've been together a long time.

TATI. At least six months.

CAROLINA. I hope one of these days I can find a guy to be with for that long.

TATI. Me too.

(*A cell phone rings.* **LIBBY** *looks at her phone.*)

CAROLINA. Who is it?

LIBBY. No one.

TATI. Gary?

LIBBY. Yeah.

CAROLINA. Answer it.

LIBBY. I'll call him back.

TATI. I'll answer it.

(**TATI** *grabs the phone.*)

LIBBY. Tati!

TATI. Hey Gary. It's Tati. Yeah, Libby's here. Just a second. It's for you.

LIBBY. Hi. Not really, just hanging out with the girls. Sure. We can work on our project. I'll be over in a while. See you soon. Bye.

CAROLINA. Did you see the way she changed when she was talking to him?

TATI. My mother's right. Here comes the bride, all dressed in white.

LIBBY. We're just friends.

CAROLINA. We know.

LIBBY. I've gotta go. We have a project due next week. We can start with the I's tomorrow?

TATI. Maybe we should stay with the G's for a while. I really like Garrett.

CAROLINA. Gerald's not my type, but I wouldn't mind dating Christopher.

(*A cell phone rings.* **LIBBY** *answers.*)

LIBBY. Oh, hi Gary. I won't forget it. Yeah. See ya'. (She hangs up) I guess it wouldn't hurt to put the club on hold for a few weeks. Gotta run.

(**LIBBY** *exits.*)

CAROLINA. No marriage before thirty?

TATI. Sure. What do you think their colors are going to be?

(*Lights down.*)

PROPS

Three notebooks and pens

THE SACRIFICE OF DATING

CHARACTERS

LESLIE

DARIA

SEBASTIAN

LAURA

SETTING

Leslie's apartment. The only furnishing on stage is Leslie's desk. On the desk is a laptop, a vase and a few magazines on love.

(**LESLIE** *sits at her desk typing on a laptop.*)

LESLIE. Why is this so hard? Open a computer and search through thousands of candidates to find the man of my dreams. Simple. Not! What I wouldn't give to have that perfect man fall right into my lap.

(**DARIA** *enters from the back of the stage.*)

DARIA. I can help you.

LESLIE. Who are you? How did you get in here?

DARIA. I'm Daria. I'm here to help you find the man of your dreams.

LESLIE. How the hell did you get in here?

DARIA. I let myself in.

LESLIE. I'm pretty sure I locked the front door. Did Jimmy give you a master key? Are you some sort of freaky plumber or something?

DARIA. I'm not a plumber, Leslie.

LESLIE. How do you know my name? You're not another stalker, are you? Listen, I'm sure you're a really good person, but I don't do women.

DARIA. I'm not a stalker either.

LESLIE. Then what are you doing here?

DARIA. I told you, I'm here to help you find the man of your dreams.

LESLIE. Sure you are. I'm going to call the police now.

DARIA. No you won't.

LESLIE. Okay, let's say you're not some freak, like that's true. How are you going to help me?

DARIA. Tell me what you want in a man and I'll deliver.

LESLIE. What's the catch?

DARIA. No catch. You write down exactly what you want in a man and I'll help you find him.

LESLIE. Laura put you up to this, didn't she? You work for that dating service.

DARIA. Here's the form. Fill it out as best you can. Here's a pen.

LESLIE. Nice pen.

DARIA. You can keep it.

LESLIE. Thanks. Where do I start?

DARIA. The top.

LESLIE. Okay. Height, five ten to six feet. Hair, brown. Athletic. This is fun. Kind of like Build a Bear except using man parts.

DARIA. Be very specific.

LESLIE. Green eyes. I love green eyes.

DARIA. Voice type?

LESLIE. Don't care.

DARIA. Country of origin?

LESLIE. Someone from another country. That's good. Let's make him British. They're so polite, not like American men.

DARIA. What about men you've dated before? Anything particular that you liked?

LESLIE. All of them had something I liked.

DARIA. Take the best of each man.

LESLIE. You must have done this before.

DARIA. Once or twice.

LESLIE. Let's see. Tony's looks. Jason's sexuality. John's creativity. Damon's financial stability. And all the fun stuff from Jeff.

DARIA. What fun stuff? Be specific.

LESLIE. I want all of his fun stuff. His sense of fun, casual demeanor and easy-going personality, all of it.

DARIA. Fair enough. Finished?

(**LESLIE** *hands* **DARIA** *the paper.*)

LESLIE. You'll never find a man this perfect.

DARIA. I already have.

LESLIE. You have?

DARIA. Yes.

LESLIE. So when can I meet this miracle man?

DARIA. Soon, but before you do, you need to be sure this is what you really want.

LESLIE. Why wouldn't I want to find the perfect man?

DARIA. The universe is made up of checks and balances. To get love, you must give love. Do you understand this?

LESLIE. Yeah.

DARIA. Then let's proceed. Type your criteria into the computer and see who comes up.

(**LESLIE** *types on the computer.*)

LESLIE. Only one profile. Sebastian Penderfeld. He's cute.

DARIA. He's perfect for you.

LESLIE. You're so confident.

DARIA. I have a remarkable matchmaking record.

LESLIE. I'm sure you do. I'll e-mail him.

DARIA. Why don't you IM him? His information is on his profile.

LESLIE. Okay.

DARIA. I'll let myself out.

LESLIE. Don't forget to send me a bill.

DARIA. This one's on the house. Good luck.

(**DARIA** *exits.*)

LESLIE. That was one weird lady. (*looking at the computer*) Sebastian's online right now. What do I write? This freaky lady told me you were my perfect mate. Not! (*typing*) 'Hi.' (*reading*) He said 'Hi' back. Now what do I write? (*typing*) 'I saw your profile and I think we have a lot in common.' (*reading*) 'Funny, I was just looking at your profile thinking the same thing.' No way! (*typing*) 'Do you want to meet for coffee?' He's British, better make that tea. (*reading*) 'I'll meet you on the corner of 17th and Green. Five minutes?' 17th and Green? That's right across the street. (*typing*) 'I'll be there.' Wait, wait, wait, wait, wait! What am I doing? Some crazy lady comes in here, tells me she's got the perfect man for me and I go running off to meet him? What have I got to lose?

(**LESLIE** *grabs her coat and runs off stage. Lights down on the desk.* **SEBASTIAN** *enters in a spotlight.* **LESLIE** *enters, looks around and sees* **SEBASTIAN**.)

LESLIE. Excuse me? Are you Sebastian?

SEBASTIAN. I am. You must be Leslie.

LESLIE. Yes.

SEBASTIAN. I...

LESLIE. This is...

SEBASTIAN. You first...

LESLIE. No please, you...

SEBASTIAN. I want you to know that I don't make a habit of spontaneously meeting woman who have plucked me from the Internet.

LESLIE. Me too. I mean, I don't just meet men on a whim. There was this woman...never mind.

SEBASTIAN. Daria?

LESLIE. You know her?

SEBASTIAN. No, I don't know her. She came to my home this morning and told me that the woman I was destined to marry would contact me this afternoon. She said the woman's name was Leslie.

LESLIE. Okay, that's creepy.

SEBASTIAN. You don't know her?

LESLIE. No. She showed up at my house ten minutes ago telling me she was going to help me find the man of my dreams. She had me fill out this form, we put some stats into the computer and you came up.

SEBASTIAN. How odd. I thought perhaps she was a prankster or trying to set me up with one of her friends, but if you don't know her...

LESLIE. I've never seen her before today. I don't even know where to find her again.

SEBASTIAN. Neither do I now that you mention it.

LESLIE. This is so strange.

SEBASTIAN. It is. What's even stranger is this feeling as if I know you.

LESLIE. You mean the overwhelming feeling that we've known each other for years?

SEBASTIAN. Yes.

LESLIE. How did she know?

SEBASTIAN. I'm not sure.

LESLIE. What do we do now?

SEBASTIAN. Would you like to have dinner with me this evening?

LESLIE. Yes.

(*Lights down.* **LESLIE** *and* **SEBASTIAN** *exit.* **LESLIE** *enters, sits at the desk and falls asleep. Lights up. There's a knock at the door.*)

Come it!

(**LAURA** *enters.*)

LAURA. You look like hell.

LESLIE. Nice to see you too.

LAURA. What's wrong with you?

LESLIE. Nothing.

LAURA. Nothing? You've never looked worse.

LESLIE. It's Sebastian.

LAURA. I knew it was too good to be true. Did he turn out to be some sort of pervert or something?

LESLIE. No, he's perfect. He's the best thing that ever happened to me. I've never been happier.

LAURA. You look miserable.

LESLIE. I am miserable.

LAURA. Back up. You're in love and life is perfect, but your miserable. I'm missing something.

LESLIE. I don't know. So many things have changed.

LAURA. Like what?

LESLIE. Before Sebastian I was thin and fit. Now look at me. I'm fat, lazy and tired.

LAURA. That's not true. You're gorgeous.

LESLIE. Look at the bags under my eyes. Look at this roll.

LAURA. You're exaggerating.

LESLIE. I'm not. Laura, he takes me to dinner every night.

LAURA. What, Taco Bell?

LESLIE. No, like steak and lobster.

LAURA. You poor thing, being treated to gourmet meals every night. I'm lucky to get McDonald's once a week.

LESLIE. But I've gained ten pounds.

LAURA. You'll run it off. You always do.

LESLIE. I can't run it off if I can't run.

LAURA. What do mean you can't run?

LESLIE. Sebastian won't let me out of bed in the mornings. He wants to cuddle.

LAURA. You know, you're not doing a very good job of gaining my sympathy here.

LESLIE. Laura, this is serious.

LAURA. Okay, so run at lunchtime and suggest sushi more often.

LESLIE. I'm not sleeping well either.

LAURA. Don't tell me, he wants to have wild, animal sex all night?

LESLIE. That's part of the problem.

LAURA. I'm leaving.

LESLIE. Laura!

LAURA. Don't mind the bitter old woman who's idea of sex is a watching a Jonny Depp movie marathon with the cat.

LESLIE. I'm sorry. I'm being selfish.

LAURA. I don't mind. Really I don't. That's what best friends are for. I'll live vicariously through your misery. Please continue.

LESLIE. I know I just sound like a whiney baby, but...

LAURA. No, I'm just jealous. Come on, tell me all about it.

LESLIE. He snores.

LAURA. Have you tried ear plugs?

LESLIE. It doesn't help. He cuddles and snores.

LAURA. Ooh. A cuddling snorer.

LESLIE. And his snoring changes every night. It's actually rather cute.

LAURA. You're obviously sleep deprived if you think his snoring is cute.

LESLIE. Well it is. Sometimes it's a low, growling snore, like this.

(**LESLIE** *imitates* **SEBASTIAN**'s *snore.*)

Then other nights it's a loud, booming snore, like this.

(**LESLIE** *imitates* **SEBASTIAN**'s *snore.*)

LAURA. Bet that rattles the windows. How was he last night?

LESLIE. A little, gurgly snore.

(**LESLIE** *imitates* **SEBASTIAN**'s *snore.*)

LAURA. Charming.

LESLIE. Sometimes he sings in his sleep. (*singing*) You see I can't smile without you...

LAURA. Okay, I get the picture. Have you tried sleeping pills?

LESLIE. Yes and they're wonderful. I'm just afraid of becoming addicted.

LAURA. How about sleeping on the couch?

LESLIE. Only when I'm desperate. He gets pouty when I sleep on the couch.

LAURA. Wish I had that problem. Most nights Joe doesn't even know I'm in the same bed with him. Hence, the Jonny Depp movies and the cat.

LESLIE. I'm sorry.

LAURA. It's really no problem. I've got a thing going with the pool boy, Javier.

LESLIE. You're cheating on Joe?

LAURA. Only in my dreams. It involves Javier, a yatch and a Hawaiian sunset.

LESLIE. Sounds perfect.

LAURA. It can't compare to your reality. You've got it good.

LESLIE. I do and he's wonderful, but I'm a wreck. What should I do?

LAURA. Trade places with me. I'll take your misery.

(DARIA *enters.*)

DARIA. Congratulations Leslie. You've found the man of your dreams.

LAURA. Who the hell are you?

LESLIE. Daria. She's the one who helped me find Sebastian.

LAURA. So you're the freaky lady. I understand now. She kinda comes out of nowhere, doesn't she?

DARIA. How's life with the perfect man?

LESLIE. Perfect. How else should it be?

DARIA. It depends on the checks and balances.

LAURA. Checks and balances?

DARIA. We all have to give up something for love.

LESLIE. Now I understand.

LAURA. I don't. Fill me in.

DARIA. What's more important to you, sleep or Sebastian?

LESLIE. Sebastian is my life.

LAURA. What's going on here?

DARIA. Are you sure?

LESLIE. Positive.

LAURA. Hello? What's going on here?

LESLIE. Daria told me the day I met Sebastian that the universe is made up of checks and balances. I didn't know what she meant until now.

LAURA. You mean that old thing that every woman turns into Roseanne Barr after two years of marriage?

LESLIE. You know about this?

LAURA. Look at me. I could be Rosanne's younger and far more beautiful sister. After 17 years of marriage I'm lucky to look this good.

LESLIE. It doesn't have to be like that.

DARIA. You have to sacrifice something for love.

LESLIE. No.

DARIA. It's the order of the universe.

(**SEBASTIAN** *enters.*)

LESLIE. Sebastian.

SEBASTIAN. Daria?

DARIA. Hello Sebastian. How's love?

SEBASTIAN. Perfect, thank you.

DARIA. Even with the drawbacks?

SEBASTIAN. Drawbacks?

DARIA. Weight gain, sleep apnea, giving up things you love.

SEBASTIAN. I wouldn't trade Leslie for anything in the world.

LESLIE. I wouldn't give up Sebastian for anything on earth.

DARIA. Even though you've both lost parts of yourselves?

LESLIE. We've gained more then we've lost.

DARIA. I can see that.

SEBASTIAN. That was cruel.

DARIA. How much would you sacrifice for love?

LESLIE. Anything. Everything.

SEBASTIAN. I'd give my life for her.

DARIA. Ah, that's what I was waiting to hear.

(**DARIA** *pulls out a gun and aims it at* **LESLIE**. **SEBASTIAN** *moves in front of* **LESLIE**.)

SEBASTIAN. Stop! What are you doing?

DARIA. Every couple I've ever paired has stayed together till death did them part and I'm going to make sure you don't ruin my record.

SEBASTIAN. You're crazy!

DARIA. Perhaps, but I'm the best matchmaker in the world.

Not one divorce, not one separation, a few arguments, but I ended them quickly.

LESLIE. I knew you were some kind of a weirdo stalker.

DARIA. I'm not a stalker. Stalkers care about the people they're stalking. I only care about my reputation. Another happy couple.

(**DARIA** *aims the gun.* **LESLIE** *pushes past* **SEBASTIAN** *and he pulls her back.*)

LESLIE. Don't hurt him!

SEBASTIAN. Leslie, get behind me!

LESLIE. I won't lose you!

SEBASTIAN. And I won't lose you!

LAURA. I won't lose either of you!

(*Laura hits* **DARIA** *over the head with a vase, takes the gun, pulls out handcuffs and begins cuffing* **DARIA.**)

LAURA. You have the right to remain silent. Anything you say can and will be used against you in a court of law. You have the right to an attorney and you're gonna need one honey. I'll see if we can get you a good psychiatrist too.

LESLIE. I can't believe you were going to kill us.

DARIA. You won't ruin my reputation!

SEBASTIAN. We love each other.

DARIA. You do now, but what about a year from now or two or five? What about the problems, the fights?

LESLIE. We'll do what other people do, work through it.

DARIA. No you won't. This is America. People don't work through their problems. They sue each other in nasty divorces to hurt the person they swore to love.

SEBASTIAN. I'm not American.

LESLIE. Which is one reason why I love him.

DARIA. You've ruined me! My career is over!

LAURA. You are one crazy lady. Come on. I have a nice doctor in a lovely cell that would like to hear all about your perfect matchmaking record.

(*Laura exits with* **DARIA**.)

LESLIE. Well, that was something else.
SEBASTIAN. Very odd indeed. Shall we nap?
LESLIE. I'd like that. I love you, Sebastian.
SEBASTIAN. I love you, Leslie.

(*Lights down.*)

PROPS

Laptop
Vase
Love magazines

NATURAL DATING

CHARACTERS

SARA

GEORGE

LESTER

SETTING

A nudist colony where the occupants observe butterflies. There are a few bushes, a tree and a large boulder. A hedge runs across the back of the stage. The bushes, boulder and hedge should be tall enough to hide the bodies of the characters and give the illusion that they are naked.

(*Lights up.* **SARA** *is hiding behind a boulder.* **GEORGE** *walks onto stage behind the bush looking for butterflies.* **SARA** *pops up, scared.*)

GEORGE. Sorry. I didn't know anyone was here.

SARA. You don't have to leave because of me.

GEORGE. Thanks. Nice grove.

SARA. It is.

GEORGE. Lots of flowers. Should attract some butterflies.

SARA. Yeah. Yeah, it should.

GEORGE. There's a Danaus gilippus.

SARA. Where?

GEORGE. Over there. There's quite a few of them here.

SARA. There are?

GEORGE. Yeah, I've seen at least three or four today.

SARA. You have?

GEORGE. Yeah, common.

SARA. Oh.

GEORGE. You come here often?

SARA. No.

GEORGE. I can't believe I just asked that question. I'm a jerk.

SARA. You're not a jerk.

GEORGE. I am.

SARA. Okay, if you say so.

GEORGE. You think I'm a jerk?

SARA. I was just agreeing with you. I don't like to argue.

GEORGE. Considerate.

SARA. Thanks.

GEORGE. I mean, dating's tough enough as it is, but like this...

SARA. Dating?

GEORGE. Not saying we are, but...

SARA. I understand.

(*pause*)

GEORGE. So, here we are.

SARA. Yeah, here we are.

GEORGE. In the raw.

SARA. Yeah, in the raw.

GEORGE. There's a Great Spangled Frittilary.

SARA. A what?

GEORGE. A Great Spangled Frittilary.

SARA. It sounds dangerous.

GEORGE. No. It's on the purple flower over there. See it? It has the orange wings and black scales on forewing veins. It's a Nymphalidae, a member of the brush-footed family, subfamily of Longwings, also known as Heliconiinae. Not many people know that.

SARA. I should probably go.

GEORGE. It was nice talking to you.

SARA. Yeah. You too.

(**LESTER** *enters behind the hedge. He's carrying a net.*)

LESTER. Sara! There you are!

SARA. Lester!

LESTER. I've been looking everywhere for you. Where have you been?

SARA. Here.

LESTER. Looking for butterflies, huh?

GEORGE. Hi.

LESTER. Hey, how's it going? I'm Lester. You two together?

SARA. Yes! This is my boyfriend, um...

GEORGE. George.

SARA. George. George, this is Lester.

GEORGE. Hi Lester.

LESTER. Hey George. You are one lucky man. I've spent a lot of time dreaming about this little muffin. Didn't know she was already taken.

SARA. Yes, the muffin's taken.

LESTER. Guess I'll have to give up on that dream then.

SARA. What a shame.

LESTER. Sorry to impose on your territory there, George.

GEORGE. No problem, Les.

LESTER. Well, happy hunting you two!

(**LESTER** *exits.*)

GEORGE. Who was that?

SARA. A stalker.

GEORGE. Ah, that explains it.

SARA. Thank you for lying for me.

GEORGE. I didn't lie. I just agreed.

SARA. Thank you for agreeing with me.

GEORGE. I don't mind helping you out. You took care of a big problem for me.

SARA. I did? What?

GEORGE. Finding a girlfriend.

SARA. Excuse me?

GEORGE. I'm kidding.

SARA. Right.

GEORGE. So how long have we been dating?

SARA. If Lester asks, we've been married for years.

GEORGE. Understood.

SARA. He's been following me around all day.

GEORGE. Creepy.

SARA. Yeah.

GEORGE. There's an Edith's Checkerspot!

SARA. That one with the white and orange spots?

GEORGE. That's her. She's beautiful, huh?

SARA. I saw one like that by the rose garden.

GEORGE. You didn't?

SARA. I did.

GEORGE. They're rare.

SARA. Actually, it might be the same one. They all look alike to me.

GEORGE. How can you say that?

SARA. I don't know a lot about butterflies.

GEORGE. Well that, my dear lady, is no ordinary butterfly. It's the rarest butterfly in the park. You're lucky to see two in one day.

SARA. Are you going to catch it?

GEORGE. No! I'm here to observe butterflies, not capture them.

SARA. I'm sorry.

GEORGE. Imagine, flying around, minding your own business when some huge net is thrown over you, trapping your wings. You struggle, trying to wriggle free, but it's no use.

SARA. Oh my!

GEORGE. Sticky, sweaty hands grab you by the wings, rubbing off the magic fairy dust that makes you fly. Your legs are bound and slowly you die of starvation or perhaps you just give up in despair knowing that you will never take flight again.

SARA. Wow!

GEORGE. And that's not the worst of it. Once your dead, your stuck through the gut with a pin onto a piece of wood, maybe even shellacked. Gives a person nightmares.

SARA. Nightmares!

GEORGE. You don't do that, do you?

SARA. No, never!

GEORGE. Glad to hear that. What do you do?

SARA. About what?

GEORGE. Work.

SARA. Oh, I work for Macy's. I'm a fashion consultant.

GEORGE. You're kidding?

SARA. No, I'm serious.

(**GEORGE** *laughs.*)

SARA. Why are you laughing?

GEORGE. Isn't that kind of an oxymoron, a nudist fashion consultant?

SARA. Well...

GEORGE. Boy, your job must be easy with everyone being naked.

SARA. Being at a nudist colony has absolutely no reflection on my ability to choose fashionable clothing.

GEORGE. Oh yeah? What are you wearing right now?

SARA. That's not a fair question.

GEORGE. Sure it is.

SARA. Honestly, I never thought I'd be caught dead in a nudist colony.

GEORGE. Could be professionally damaging.

SARA. Makes me nervous.

GEORGE. I'm a little nervous too. You know, the whole nude thing.

SARA. You seem so confident.

GEORGE. Only when it comes to butterflies. It doesn't mean I don't get nervous about other things.

SARA. Like what?

GEORGE. Like...so how about those Giants?

SARA. Those giant what?

GEORGE. The baseball team.

SARA. Just kidding. I know who they are.

GEORGE. That's good. I could never date a woman who didn't know who the Giant's are.

SARA. Date?

GEORGE. Not that I'm saying we're...

SARA. Yeah.

GEORGE. Look, there's another Queen.

SARA. Another what?

GEORGE. Danaus gilippus.

SARA. Of course.

GEORGE. Beautiful.

SARA. Excuse me?

GEORGE. The butterfly.

SARA. Right.

GEORGE. Look at those wings. The colors.

SARA. I could never be a butterfly.

GEORGE. Why not?

SARA. It would be boring wearing the same old wings every-day. I can't even wear the same earrings two days in a row.

GEORGE. Your earrings are nice.

SARA. Thanks. They're designer, unique. I like to be different.

GEORGE. Like butterflies.

SARA. They all look the same to me.

GEORGE. They're not.

SARA. I can't tell, but if I was a butterfly I would want to break out of that mold. Be me.

GEORGE. What and have a blue mohawk like my nephew?

SARA. Why not? And different wings for each day of the week, just for a change.

GEORGE. There's a Nymphalis californica. She's perfect too!

SARA. How do you know it's a she?

GEORGE. She's flying crooked. Obviously a woman driver.

SARA. That's not nice.

GEORGE. Just joking. At this time of day only the ladies are flying. The men are hanging out in the trees, checking out the ladies.

SARA. You're lying.

GEORGE. Nope. The boys are hanging out, having a few licks of pollen with their buddies, watching the game, checking out the chicks.

SARA. Then what are the ladies doing?

GEORGE. Shopping. For different wings. At Macy's.

SARA. You're making fun of me.

GEORGE. No. Okay, yes.

SARA. What are the females really doing?

GEORGE. Eating, enjoying the scenery, looking for men. Lounge time doesn't vary much between species.

SARA. You must be scientist. You know so much about butterflies.

GEORGE. No. I'm a gynecologist.

SARA. A gyne...

GEORGE. Okay, I'm not a gynecologist. I just thought it would be a funny answer.

SARA. You're a professional liar.

GEORGE. I'm a comedian.

SARA. Sure.

GEORGE. No. I'm actually a comedian.

SARA. If you're really a comedian, say something funny.

GEORGE. What do mean, say something funny? I can't just say funny things. I have a routine. I have writers.

SARA. You don't write your own material?

GEORGE. Most of it, but I have other people tell me whether or not it's actually funny.

SARA. Well try to think of something funny and I'll tell you if it is.

GEORGE. It's not that easy.

SARA. I didn't think being a comedian was that hard.

GEORGE. There's a lot of pressure. People think you have to be funny all the time.

SARA. You don't have to be funny with me. You can just be you.

GEORGE. Are you saying I'm not funny?

SARA. No, I'm just saying I like you, funny or not.

GEORGE. Thanks. I like you too. Listen, I have to be honest with you. I'm not really...holy Ridings' Satyr, it's a Glaucopsyche lygdamus, the Silvery Blue.

SARA. A what?

GEORGE. The Silvery Blue! They're thought to be extinct.

SARA. Are you sure?

GEORGE. Very sure. I've gotta take a picture of it. Keep an eye on it. Don't let it out of your sight.

SARA. I don't know if I can.

(**GEORGE** *ducks behind the shrub. He comes back up with a camera.*)

SARA. I don't mean to be personal, but where were you carrying that camera?

GEORGE. In the camera bag.

SARA. Of course.

GEORGE. The Silvery Blue! Where did it go?

SARA. I don't know.

GEORGE. There it is. Help me get a picture of it.

SARA. George, I can't.

GEORGE. Sara, now is not the time to be shy. This is the scientific discovery of the century.

SARA. But George, I haven't been honest with you.

GEORGE. What, do you have three legs or something?

SARA. No, worse.

GEORGE. Worse than three legs?

SARA. I'm...

GEORGE. You have leprosy?

SARA. No. I'm disease free.

GEORGE. That's a relief. Then what? Wait, where did it go?

(**SARA** *steps from behind the rock. She is wearing shorts and a strapless shirt. She has the Silvery Blue on her shoulder.*)

SARA. I'm clothed.

GEORGE. Stop!

SARA. I'm sorry.

GEORGE. Hold very, very still!

SARA. What are you going to do to me?

GEORGE. The Silvery Blue is on your shoulder!

SARA. What? Get it off of me!

GEORGE. Sara, hold still!

SARA. I hate bugs!

GEORGE. Butterflies aren't bugs!

SARA. Is it going to bite me?

GEORGE. Butterflies don't bite!

SARA. Are you sure?

GEORGE. Yes! Sara, please just hold very still. I have to take a picture.

SARA. Don't come out!

(**SARA** *covers her eyes.* **GEORGE** *comes out from behind the rock. He's dressed in a pair of Bermuda shorts.* **GEORGE** *takes a picture of the butterfly.*)

GEORGE. Got it!

(**SARA** *runs back behind the rock.*)

GEORGE. What are you doing?

SARA. Hiding.

GEORGE. Why?

SARA. I'm embarrassed.

GEORGE. Sara, you have clothes on.

SARA. You don't.

GEORGE. Yes, I do.

SARA. You do?

GEORGE. Look.

(**SARA** *peaks over the top of the rock.*)

SARA. You're wearing shorts.

GEORGE. Is it that obvious?

(**SARA** *ducks back behind the rock.*)

GEORGE. Sara?

SARA. I lied to you.

GEORGE. I lied to you too.

SARA. I lied to you more. I hate bugs, I hate butterflies,

I hate being naked and I hate other people being naked.

GEORGE. You hate butterflies? How can you hate butterflies?

SARA. They scare me.

GEORGE. Scare you? Oh Sara, you poor girl. Come on out.

SARA. You don't understand.

GEORGE. It's all right. I'll protect you.

SARA. I can't be here. At this place. My job is to make people look good. Everyone here is the same.

GEORGE. We're not all the same. We're all very different.

SARA. I don't see that.

GEORGE. Then why are you talking to me instead of Lester?

SARA. Because you're not a stalker.

GEORGE. Are you sure? I'm kidding. Look, I'm talking to you because you're different, different than all those other naked women.

SARA. Are you trying to be funny?

GEORGE. Yes. Is it working?

SARA. A little.

GEORGE. Good. Come out.

(**SARA** *comes out.*)

SARA. Was that butterfly really extinct?

GEORGE. It was thought to be. You'll be famous. Hey, don't forget about us little people, okay?

SARA. You spotted it. You took the picture.

GEORGE. I couldn't have done it without your shoulder.

(*offstage*)

LESTER. Sara!

SARA. Not again.

GEORGE. Do you know Photoshop?

SARA. Yes. Why?

GEORGE. I don't want to be forward, but would you like to go download these pictures with me?

SARA. I don't know.

GEORGE. It's not like it's a date or anything. It's all in the interest of the Silvery Blue.

(*offstage*)

LESTER. Sara!

GEORGE. What have you got to lose?

(*offstage*)

LESTER. Sara!

SARA. Nothing. Let's go.

(*They start to leave, but* **SARA** *stops* **GEORGE.**)

You're a nice person, George.

GEORGE. Nice? I'm supposed to be funny. I'll have to talk to my writers about that.

(*As they run off stage we see the Silvery Blue is on* **SARA**'s *back.* **LESTER** *enters with his butterfly net.*)

LESTER. Sara?

(*Lights down.*)

PROPS

Camera
Butterfly Net
Butterfly

POST DATING

LES
CHARLIE
ETHEL
BOB

SETTING

A small, old-fashioned post office in an out of the way town. Cubby holes are stage left, a counter runs vertical down the center of the stage and two stools are between the counter and the cubby holes.

(**LES** *is putting mail into the cubby holes.* **CHARLIE** *is sitting on a stool.*)

LES. You should have seen me in my younger days. They called me Mr. Romance.

CHARLIE. Mr. Romance?

LES. The ladies couldn't resist me.

(*looking at a letter*)

Ah, Haddie Henderson. Now she was a beauty back in high school. Straight A student too. She was something else. We went out during my sophomore year. I remember it like it was yesterday.

CHARLIE. What happened with Haddie?

LES. I got bored. They all bored me sooner or later.

CHARLIE. That why you ain't never been married?

LES. Never found the right woman. I have pretty high standards, you know.

CHARLIE. There must have been one special lady.

LES. They were all special, if you know what I mean.

(*looking at another letter*)

Susie Churchill. Became a fashion model. Married some stock broker in New York. She was gorgeous.

CHARLIE. I remember her. She's beautiful.

LES. But dumb as stale bread. Nothin' but a trophy wife.

CHARLIE. A trophy wife?

LES. That's what they call a beautiful women that marries a rich man, like they're some kind of prize or something. Not for me. Give me a faithful, homely woman any day of the week. Okay, maybe not homely, but faithful.

(*looking at a letter*)

Mandy Brown. Does that name bring back memories.

CHARLIE. Ms. Brown, the librarian?

LES. The librarian and you know what they say about librarians?

CHARLIE. They're smart and organized.

LES. No. They're hiding something.

CHARLIE. I didn't know librarians were so secretive.

LES. They are. Every day they put on their little librarian outfits and walk around being quiet and respectable, but get 'em alone and they unleash their inner animal.

CHARLIE. Animal? Do they get mean?

LES. Mean? You should see 'em. Claws out to here. Eyes wild with desire. See this scar? That was from Mary Beth White, Reference Department at State. And this one, Corinne LaRue, a French foreign exchange student studying library sciences in New Mexico.

CHARLIE. Wow!

LES. Mr. Romance. Hey, let me teach you a little trick.

CHARLIE. Okay.

LES. I can unsnap a woman's bra in less than five seconds.

CHARLIE. No!

LES. Watch this.

(*yelling*)

Package pickup.

(**ETHEL** *enters with a cart.*)

ETHEL. Hello Les. Hello Charlie. Are you learning anything?

(**LES** *reaches behind* **ETHEL** *and snaps open her bra.* **ETHEL** *reaches back and casually rehooks it.*)

No package?

LES. I've got a package for you Ethel.

ETHEL. Honey, I saw that package when it was in its prime. No interest now. Charlie, you watch yourself with this one. He's dangerous.

CHARLIE. Yes ma'm.

(**ETHEL** *exits.*)

LES. That must have been four seconds. I haven't lost it.

CHARLIE. Teach me how to do it.

LES. Sure kid. It's a snap.

(**LES** *snaps his fingers.*)

CHARLIE. A snap.

LES. Just snap your fingers.

CHARLIE. Like this?

(**CHARLIE** *tries to snap his fingers.*)

LES. Close, but it might be easier if we try it at the source.

(**LES** *reaches under the counter, pulls out a bra and puts it on.*)

I call this my training bra. Okay, now get behind me and put your fingers on the hook. Got it?

CHARLIE. I think so.

LES. What do you mean you think so? Do you have your hand on the hooks or not?

CHARLIE. I don't know. What do they look like?

LES. Son, haven't you seen a bra before?

CHARLIE. Sure I have. Every day. My mom hangs her bras on the kitchen chairs to dry.

LES. That's exciting. Have you ever seen a bra on a woman before?

CHARLIE. I've seen them on a manikin.

(**LES** *takes off the bra.*)

LES. Looks like we have to start with bra basics 101. These are the straps, these are the cups and these are the ever-important hooks. Got that?

CHARLIE. Straps, cups, hooks.

LES. Now, the cups hold the precious cargo. Slide down the straps for limited breast access from above.

CHARLIE. Breast?

LES. If she lets you slide down a strap she may let you go for the gold, but she'll make you work for it so the best access is through the Mr. Romance snap. Let's try it.

(**LES** *takes a brown wrapped package from under the counter. He puts the package on the counter and fastens the bra around the package.*)

CHARLIE. I don't know if I can.

LES. Of course you can. Watch closely and learn.

(*to the package*)

You are, without a doubt, the most beautiful woman I have ever seen.

(*to* **CHARLIE**)

This part's important.

(*to the package*)

I love you.

(**LES** *leans in as if to kiss the package, reaches around and undoes the snap.* **BOB** *walks in the front door.*)

BOB. She's one of your better looking dates, Les.

LES. Just showing the kid my technique.

(**LES** *fastens the bra back onto the package.*)

BOB. Of course. The best way to learn about girls is from a man who kisses boxes wrapped in women's bras.

LES. I was teaching the pup the snap.

BOB. Ah, the Mr. Romance snap. You taught that to every kid in school. There wasn't a safe bra in Valley High.

LES. There were a few safe bras. Not everyone got it. Remember Simon Lowry?

BOB. Poor kid. He never quite got the hang of it, but that didn't stop him from trying.

LES. You remember that time he tried to snap Charlene Dale's bra?

BOB. Do I? It was cold outside and Simon was wearing these gloves with hooks on them. You know, the kind you can hook together so you don't lose one?

CHARLIE. I have some of those.

BOB. Me too.

LES. He put his hand up to snap Charlene's bra and got that hook stuck on her sweater.

CHARLIE. You mean stuck stuck or just stuck?

BOB. Oh no, he was stuck like a chicken in a wire fence.

CHARLIE. Poor Simon!

CHARLIE. That wasn't the half of it. Charlene's boyfriend, Bruno, saw it and started chasin' Simon.

CHARLIE. Did he catch him?

BOB. Not a chance. Simon was stuck on Charlene's sweater.

LES. He tried to get away, though. He dodged this way and that. But she went one way and he went another and that sweater ripped clean off her back!

CHARLIE. You means she was naked?

BOB. Close enough.

CHARLIE. What did he do?

LES. Simon took off like a jack rabbit and never came back to school.

CHARLIE. Poor Simon.

BOB. He became a priest.

LES. At the Lady of the Sacred Cross Your Heart.

CHARLIE. What about Charlene?

BOB. Poor girl. Once she lost her sweater everyone could see that she stuffed her bra with old nylons. Flat as a pancake.

LES. She got a breast enlargement and became a Dallas Cowboy Cheerleader.

BOB. That girl really knew how to bounce.

LES. She did. Need your mail, Bob?

BOB. Well, this is a post office isn't it?

LES. Charlie, can you go into the back and get the morning mail?

CHARLIE. Sure.

(**CHARLIE** *exits.* **LES** *starts to put the package under the counter.*)

BOB. Can I give it a shot before you put it away?

LES. Be my guest.

(*to the package*)

BOB. You are one of the most beautiful women I have ever seen. I love you.

(**BOB** *reaches behind the box and struggles to snap the hook.*)

LES. All those years of married life have taken the snap right out of you.

BOB. I'm just a little rusty. Here, hold the box. It needs to be the right height.

LES. Sure Bob.

(**LES** *holds the box for* **BOB**.)

BOB. I'm ready now.

(*to the box*)

Baby, you've got the most beautiful lips. I love you.

(**BOB** *reaches around the box and struggles to snap the hooks.* **ETHEL** *walks in and takes the package.*)

ETHEL. This package needs to get on the truck.

(*As she's walking away with the package* **LES** *snaps the hook on her bra.* **ETHEL** *stops, sighs and exits.*)

BOB. You are the man. That must have been three seconds.

LES. I still got it.

(**ETHEL** *walks back on stage with the bra from the box and hands it to* **LES**.)

ETHEL. There's no postage on this.

(**ETHEL** *exits.*)

BOB. She wants you.

LES. She's had me, again and again and again.

BOB. I always thought you would end up with Ethel.

LES. You gotta be kidding me?

BOB. What's wrong with her?

LES. Nothing's wrong with her it's just...

BOB. Not up to your standards?

LES. Naw. We just have different views on things.

BOB. Like marriage?

LES. Yeah. She wanted to get married and I didn't.

BOB. Well, it worked out for both of you. She has a nice family and you have the post office.

(**CHARLIE** *enters with a bin full of mail and puts it on the counter.*)

LES. I still have my reputation. You admire me, don't you Charlie?

CHARLIE. Yes, sir.

LES. See.

BOB. I'm happy for you, Les. Well, I've gotta get home to Betsy.

CHARLIE. Your wife?

BOB. Yes Charlie and a heck of a wife she is. She's one of the few women in town who was never romanced by Mr. Romance here.

LES. Not that I didn't try.

(**LES** *hands* **BOB** *his mail.*)

BOB. But I had a lot of romance of my own to sway her.

LES. She just felt sorry for you.

BOB. I'll give her your best, Les. Bye Charlie.

CHARLIE. Bye.

(**BOB** *exits.* **LES** *watches.*)

CHARLIE. You can still get married.

LES. What? Why would you think I want to get married?

CHARLIE. Everyone wants to grow old with someone.

LES. I'm already old.

CHARLIE. You're not that old. And you've still got it, right? Mr. Romance.

LES. Yeah Charlie, Mr. Romance. The stamp machine in the back needs refilling. Can you take care of that for me?

CHARLIE. Sure.

(**CHARLIE** *exits.* **LES** *takes a few letters and starts sorting them into the cubby holes. He looks at each one carefully and thinks about it before putting it into the hole.* **ETHEL** *enters with a couple of small packages.*)

ETHEL. Two more packages for the newlyweds on Parker Street. Boy, they sure did get a lot of presents for their wedding.

LES. They're Jewish, aren't they?

ETHEL. Yup and what a beautiful wedding. Masel tov!

(**ETHEL** *starts to leave.*)

LES. How are the kids?

ETHEL. Good. Mark's practice is coming along. He just got his first big client and Keily's baby just turned two. Ah, you should see her. What an angel! I wish her grandpa could be here.

LES. Charlie's doing a good job. He's a hard worker.

ETHEL. He's a good boy. His dad would be proud.

LES. His mom should be proud.

ETHEL. I'm proud of all my kids.

LES. Yeah.

ETHEL. You should of had kids, Les.

LES. They wouldn't fit in my life.

ETHEL. No room between the women, the parties and the bars? Guess it's a trade off.

(**ETHEL** *starts to leave again.*)

LES. What are you doing after work?

ETHEL. Charlie and I are going to a movie. You wanna come?

LES. I don't wanna butt in.

ETHEL. You're always welcome.

LES. You gonna see some chick flick?

ETHEL. We're seeing that new horror film about the woman who kills all her husbands in really gruesome ways. Come with us.

LES. Do you remember when we would go to the football field, sit on the bleachers and drink lemon gin till the sun came up?

ETHEL. That was a long time ago.

LES. How about we drop Charlie off at home and you and I go relive those days?

ETHEL. You can't relive the past Lester.

LES. Lester? You haven't called me that in years.

ETHEL. You're a sweet, charming, dear man, but my son and I have a date tonight. You can come with us, but I'm not standing him up.

LES. It's only one night.

ETHEL. Another time.

LES. Ethel, I miss you.

ETHEL. You see me everyday.

LES. And every day for the past twenty-seven years I've watched you build a life.

ETHEL. I'm blessed.

LES. You are and in you I see the mistakes of my past.

ETHEL. They weren't mistakes, Les. You are who you are. You're a free spirit.

LES. I'm a free spirit who's afraid to die alone.

ETHEL. You won't be alone. You have so many friends.

LES. Big Charlie was lucky to have you there when he passed.

ETHEL. He was a good man. I have to get back to work. The afternoon truck will be here soon.

LES. Ethel, I know it hasn't been long since Charlie passes, but, do you think maybe you would consider going on a date with me?

ETHEL. You're a little out of my league Les. I'm a nice girl, remember?

LES. I remember. You're the finest woman I've ever known. I promise no hanky panky or snapping bras. Just dinner. Okay, maybe a kiss or two.

ETHEL. Another time Les.

(**ETHEL** *exits.* **CHARLIE** *enters.*)

CHARLIE. I filled up the postage machine.

LES. Thanks Charlie. You know, that's quite a mom you've got there.

CHARLIE. Yeah. She thinks a lot of you too.

LES. She does?

CHARLIE. Says you've got a real good heart and it's a shame you never settled down and had some kids. Says you're good breeding stock.

LES. She said that about me?

CHARLIE. Yep.

(*looking off stage*)

Afternoon mail truck's here. Should I take out the bins?

LES. Thanks Charlie.

(**CHARLIE** *exits.* **LES** *looks at a few more letters and looks off stage. He smiles.*)

(*reading an envelope*)

Karen Molinado. Now that was a girl with huge personality.

(*Lights down.*)

PROPS

Several envelopes of all sizes

Small mail bin

A woman's bra

Large box wrapped in brown paper large enough on which
to fasten the bra

Push cart

PRE-DATING

CHARACTERS

NOLO

ARG

NALA

CREBO

SETTING

Inside a cave in the prehistoric era.

(**NOLO** *sits in the middle of the floor working on a large, round, flat stone that looks like a wheel.* **ARG** *enters.*)

ARG. Hi Nolo.

NOLO. Hey Arg.

ARG. Wow! Look at all this stuff!

NOLO. I've been busy.

ARG. I can see that. All this for Nala?

NOLO. Yeah. Do you think she'll like it?

ARG. What is it?

NOLO. I call it art.

ARG. Art. What do you do with it?

NOLO. It's supposed to make you feel something.

ARG. Hey, sounds like fun.

NOLO. It is. Here, look at this. No, really look at it. Do you feel anything?

ARG. A little dizzy.

NOLO. Good. It made you feel something. That's the whole purpose of art.

ARG. It definitely made me feel dizzy.

NOLO. Then it's working.

ARG. What are you making there?

NOLO. I call it round.

ARG. Nice.

NOLO. It's my favorite piece so far.

ARG. I can see why.

NOLO. I hope Nala will like it. Have you seen her?

ARG. She was hunting with Crebo.

NOLO. What does she see in that Neanderthal?

ARG. You mean besides the muscles, good looks and extraordinary hunting skills?

NOLO. Okay, so he can track and trap. But can he make art?

ARG. No, I'm pretty sure he can't make art.

NOLO. Ha!

ARG. In fact, I don't know anyone else that can make the things that you can. You're one of a kind.

NOLO. Thanks Arg.

ARG. So what do you do with round?

NOLO. Well, you can lean it against a wall and look at it.

ARG. Is that all?

NOLO. It's art. It's just supposed to make you feel something.

ARG. Okay.

(**NALA** *is heard offstage.*)

NOLO. There's Nala.

(**NOLO** *runs to the side of the stage. He yells and waves.*)

Hi Nala!

ARG. Poor schlep.

NOLO. Hm?

ARG. Nothing.

NOLO. Did you see her? She's so...so...

(*picking up an object*)

She's so bondo.

ARG. Bondo? What's bondo?

NOLO. This is bondo. Words can't describe Nala, only art.

ARG. You've got it bad, don't you?

(**NALA** *enters. She carries a spear.*)

NALA. Hi Arg. Hi Nolo.

ARG. Hi Nala. How's hunting?

NALA. Crebo caught big deer and small birds for tonight.

ARG. My favorite.

NOLO. Great.

NALA. What's that?

NOLO. Bondo.

NALA. What's bondo?

ARG. It's you.

NALA. What?

NOLO. It's art. Something that I created. It's supposed to make you feel something.

NALA. How does it do that? Do you rub it on your skin? Hit yourself in the head? Put it in your shirt?

ARG. Oh my...

NOLO. You can do all of those things with bondo if that's how it makes you feel. I like to look at it and hold it.

NALA. What's this?

NOLO. It's round.

NALA. What do you do with round?

NOLO. Look at it.

(*Looking at it.*)

NALA. What's it gonna do?

NOLO. Nothing. Just look at it. Really look at it. How does it make you feel?

NALA. A little dizzy.

ARG. Me too.

NOLO. Then it made you feel. That's what art is supposed to do.

NALA. Oh.

(*offstage*)

CREBO. Nala!

NALA. I have to go help with food. Bye Nolo. Bye Arg.

(**NALA** *exits.*)

(**NOLO** *speaks offstage after* **NALA**.)

NOLO. They're all for you. Everything I do I do for you. Everything I make I make for you.

ARG. She's gone.

NOLO. I know. I could never say those things to her face.

ARG. Why not? Maybe she'll say nice things back.

NOLO. Maybe she'll laugh.

ARG. Hey, if she didn't laugh at bondo and round.

NOLO. She did like them, didn't she?

ARG. She was being polite.

NOLO. Maybe the round can be better.

ARG. I think it's good just the way it is. Can I have it?

NOLO. I want to work more with this one. You can have the first one I made.

ARG. You made another one?

(**NOLO** *gets another round.*)

NOLO. It's not perfect.

ARG. What's that thing coming out of it?

NOLO. It looked a little plain so I made a hole in the center, but didn't like the hole so I plugged it with a stick.

ARG. The stick adds a lot.

NOLO. Eh, I don't like it now. You can have it.

ARG. Hey, look what I can do.

(**ARG** *spins the round like a top.*)

NOLO. Can you do that someplace else? I've gotta get back to work.

ARG. For a man in love you are far too serious.

NOLO. Love. Why can't Nala love me?

ARG. Because she's infatuated with Crebo's good looks and muscles.

NOLO. I'm sure she appreciates my creativity.

ARG. Creativity doesn't feed the tribe.

NOLO. But look at this. Doesn't it make you feel good?

ARG. Still makes me queasy.

NOLO. I made this out of nothing and it makes me feel stronger then killing a bull.

ARG. Then I say you do it. Nala will learn to love it.

NOLO. Maybe. Maybe I'm just a fool.

ARG. I don't believe that. I think you've got talent and one of these days you're going to be famous. And when that day comes I'm going to have a collection of all your stuff.

NOLO. It's not stuff, it's art.

ARG. Hey, what's this?

NOLO. I call it fire.

ARG. What are these rocks?

NOLO. Don't touch those. Each one is perfectly placed.

ARG. Sorry. I didn't know there was an order to the rocks.

NOLO. Of course there's an order. It's art.

(**NALA** *enters.*)

NALA. I forgot my spear. What are you looking at?

NOLO. Nala!

NALA. Of course you're looking at Nala, but what is that?

NOLO. I call it fire.

(**NALA** *picks up a stone and inspects it.*)

ARG. You shouldn't touch those. They're perfectly placed.

NALA. Huh?

NOLO. Nothing. You can do whatever you like with the rock. You can keep it if you want.

NALA. Nala has many rocks.

(**NALA** *tosses the rock back into the stick and wood mixture. It sparks and then starts smoking.*)

ARG. What the...?

NALA. Did I break fire?

NOLO. I don't know.

(**NOLO** *reaches for the bowl.*)

Ow! It hurts, like the sun.

ARG. Let me feel.

(**ARG** *touches the fire.*)

Holy buffalo breath, that hurts! I think we're on to something here.

NALA. I'm sorry I ruined fire.

NOLO. You didn't ruin anything.

ARG. Look at this. I'm making my own art.

(**ARG** *is playing with the smoke.*)

NOLO. You probably made it better. Look, it's much better.

(**NALA** *gets close to the fire and starts coughing.*)

NALA. Nala feels something.

(**NALA** *faints.*)

NOLO. Nala!

ARG. Great, you killed her with art.

NOLO. Help me put her on the round.

(**NOLO** *and* **ARG** *carry* **NALA** *and place her on the round with the stick in the middle.*)

The other round.

ARG. This art could come in handy. We wouldn't have to hit the girls over the head anymore. Just show them fire.

NOLO. You don't really hit girls over the head, do you?

ARG. Don't you?

NOLO. No.

ARG. That explains why I don't have many dates.

(**NALA** *wakes.*)

NOLO. Nala, are you okay?

NALA. Nolo, how did you do that?

NOLO. I don't know.

NALA. Art has great power. We must tell the others.

NOLO. Oh no.

NALA. But art can be used to trap animals.

NOLO. Art shouldn't be used to hurt things.

NALA. You will be known as a great hunter.

NOLO. That's not what I made it for.

ARG. Hold on a second. You're telling Nala that you won't let her use art for hunting? You must be serious about this art stuff.

NOLO. It's not stuff. It's meant to make you feel good, not to hurt things.

NALA. But it is better to get animals. Now we kill them with spears. Art would make them sleep.

ARG. Nala's got something there. It would be much kinder to the little animals. Just let us try it. If you don't like it, we won't do it again.

NOLO. Well, I guess.

(ARG *picks up fire.*)

ARG. Great! Here you go Nala. Make sure to tell everyone it was made by Nolo.

NALA. Nala will.

(NALA *exits.*)

ARG. Oh Nolo, you're gonna be famous! Everyone will know how brilliant you are.

NOLO. I don't think it's right to hurt things with art. Art is meant to make you feel good, not bad.

(*A scream is heard outside.* NALA *runs in.*)

ARG. What's happening?

NALA. Crebo is fire. He screams and rolls on the ground.

NOLO. What do you mean Crebo is fire?

NALA. I gave Crebo fire and told him how it made me sleep. He put fire on rabbit to make it sleep. Rabbit turned into fire and began running through the village. Everything it ran past became fire. All of the huts fall to the ground. Crebo jumped on rabbit to stop it and Crebo became fire.

ARG. Uh oh.

NOLO. Where is Crebo now?

NALA. He fell in river and fire stopped. He is angry and wants to know where fire came from.

ARG. Did you tell him Nolo made it?

NALA. You said tell everyone Nolo made it so Nala did.

NOLO. I'm dead.

ARG. Well, you didn't know your art would destroy the village and take down the biggest guy in the tribe. Wait, you destroyed a whole village and took down the biggest guy in the tribe. I think we've got something here.

NOLO. I told you art is for good, not bad.

ARG. But look at the big picture. We could beat any other tribe. We could get any animal. We could rule the world.

NALA. Nolo is powerful.

NOLO. He is?

NALA. Nala thinks Nolo should be tribe leader.

NOLO. He should?

NALA. Nolo much smarter than Crebo.

NOLO. I am?

NALA. Nolo should be leader.

NOLO. No, no, no. I don't want to be leader. I'm just an artist.

ARG. Come on buddy. This is your big shot. Don't walk away from destiny.

NOLO. Listen, it's nice that you want me to be the leader, but I'll leave that to Crebo.

(**CREBO** *enters carrying a charred rabbit.*)

CREBO. Nolo!

NOLO. Crebo!

ARG. Hey Crebo. You're looking mighty manly today.

(**CREBO** *growls at* **ARG.**)

CREBO. Crebo have problem with art. Art make Crebo burn like sun. Crebo want to make Nolo burn like sun.

ARG. I wouldn't mess with Nolo if I were you.

CREBO. Why not?

ARG. Nolo has some pretty powerful art. He destroyed the village without even being there and look what he did to this little bunny.

NOLO. Poor rabbit.

(ARG *takes the rabbit from* CREBO. *He sniffs it.*)

ARG. This smells pretty good.

(ARG *takes a bite of the rabbit.*)

ARG (CONT'D). Wow! This is fantastic! Take a bite of this.

(ARG *hands the rabbit to* NALA. *She bites the rabbit.*)

NALA. Best food Nala ever had. Try Crebo.

(CREBO *takes the rabbit and bites. He likes it and begins hungrily eating the rest.*)

ARG. I wonder what would happen if we used fire on, say, buffalo?

NALA. Or bird?

CREBO. Crebo like fire. It makes food taste good. Nolo make more.

NOLO. I can't.

CREBO. What mean you can't?

ARG. He means that he can't while you're watching. It's a secret.

NOLO. No. I mean I don't know how.

CREBO. You make first time. Do again.

NOLO. I made art. Nala made fire.

CREBO. Nala make fire? Do again.

NALA. I don't know how.

ARG. I think I do. It takes both Nolo and Nala to make fire. Nala, where's art?

NALA. Crebo threw onto rabbit.

ARG. Can you find art and bring it back?

CREBO. Crebo get art.

(CREBO *exits.*)

NOLO. What are you doing?

ARG. Taste that rabbit. It's good. Imagine, no more cold slimy food. We can use fire on everything.

NOLO. No! We're not going to make fire again. Fire hurts. It's bad.

NALA. Fire is good. Rabbit tastes better.

NOLO. Look what it did to the village.

ARG. Those huts were old. They needed renovation anyway.

(**CREBO** *enters again with art.*)

CREBO. Make fire.

ARG. Give me art. Nolo, can you arrange the rocks the way you had them before.

NOLO. No.

ARG. Oh, come on. Just put the rocks in the special order.

NOLO. No.

ARG. Please?

NALA. For Nala?

NOLO. Oh all right. For Nala.

(**NOLO** *arranges the rocks.*)

ARG. Nala, which rock did you pick up?

NALA. This one.

ARG. Okay, pick it up and throw it back in the pile again like you did before.

(**NALA** *picks up a rock and tosses it into the art. Nothing happens.*)

Are you sure this is the way the rocks were before?

NOLO. Yes.

ARG. And that was the rock you picked up and threw?

NALA. Yes.

ARG. Try again.

(**NALA** *tries again, but nothing.*)

CREBO. Crebo thinks Nolo and Nala lie. Fire came from someplace else. Crebo go look for fire.

(**CREBO** *exits.*)

NALA. Nala sad. Rabbit taste good. Nala want more. Nala go cry.

(**NALA** *exits.*)

ARG. Well, that fame was short lived. Guess I'll take my round and go home. Oh, wait. I don't have a home anymore. It burned down. Looks like I'll go build a new home. Keep working on that art, Nolo. Maybe one day you'll make something that'll be useful.

NOLO. Maybe.

(**ARG** *exits.* **NOLO** *opens his hand to reveal another rock. He looks at it for a moment, looks at fire, tosses the rock onto the pile and it starts smoking.* **NOLO** *smiles. Lights down.*)

PROPS

Two rounds, one with a stick through the center
Bondo
Pile of rocks and sticks for fire
Spear
Charred rabbit

DATING SERVICE

CHARACTERS

MISS RIGHT
CHARLOTTE
DANNY WRONG

SETTING

The Right Place, an exclusive dating service.

(**MISS RIGHT** *sits at a desk doing paperwork.* **CHAR-LOTTE** *enters.*)

MISS RIGHT. Can I help you?

CHARLOTTE. I'm looking for Miss Right.

MISS RIGHT. I'm Miss Right.

CHARLOTTE. I wasn't sure that I was in The Right Place.

MISS RIGHT. You are in the The Right Place. Sit. Sit.

CHARLOTTE. Thank you.

MISS RIGHT. How can I help you?

CHARLOTTE. I'd like to find Mr. Right.

MISS RIGHT. Then you're definitely in the right place. We have all the right men for all the right ladies.

CHARLOTTE. I'm sure you're right.

MISS RIGHT. I'm always right. Now, tell me what you are looking for in the right man?

CHARLOTTE. I'd like someone who is average in height.

MISS RIGHT. Not too tall, not too short, but right in the middle?

CHARLOTTE. Yes, that's right.

MISS RIGHT. What about hair?

CHARLOTTE. Any hair color is all right, but the length should be right about here.

MISS RIGHT. Right about here?

CHARLOTTE. Yes, that's right.

MISS RIGHT. Eyes?

CHARLOTTE. Right now I like men with blue eyes.

MISS RIGHT. Blue eyes, right, but for Mr. Right will any shade be all right?

CHARLOTTE. Of course, any shade would be all right for Mr. Right.

MISS RIGHT. All right.

CHARLOTTE. He should be laid back. Not too lazy, not too driven.

MISS RIGHT. Right.

CHARLOTTE. He shouldn't be boring. He should love excitement.

MISS RIGHT. Right on the edge.

CHARLOTTE. Yes.

MISS RIGHT. But still casual.

CHARLOTTE. Right on.

MISS RIGHT. Political views?

CHARLOTTE. Right wing.

MISS RIGHT. Of course. Any preference on employment?

CHARLOTTE. I'd like a writer.

MISS RIGHT. A writer?

CHARLOTTE. Yes.

MISS RIGHT. What type of writing do you like?

CHARLOTTE. Writing from right around the turn of the century.

MISS RIGHT. I know the right man. He lives right around the corner.

CHARLOTTE. Is he a writer?

MISS RIGHT. Yes.

CHARLOTTE. Right wing?

MISS RIGHT. That's right.

CHARLOTTE. Lives right on the edge?

MISS RIGHT. With the right attitude.

CHARLOTTE. Is he righteous?

MISS RIGHT. Right as rain.

CHARLOTTE. Looking for the right woman.

MISS RIGHT. Right now.

CHARLOTTE. Perhaps I could write him an e-mail.

MISS RIGHT. We have to find out first if you're right for him.

CHARLOTTE. All right.

MISS RIGHT. He wants a woman who is right about your height, maybe taller.

CHARLOTTE. I can be taller with the right shoes.

MISS RIGHT. What type of shoes?

CHARLOTTE. Nothing but Wright shoes.

MISS RIGHT. Do you live in the right neighborhood?

CHARLOTTE. I'm right across from Central Park.

MISS RIGHT. And your home?

CHARLOTTE. Frank Lloyd Wright, of course.

MISS RIGHT. Favorite song?

CHARLOTTE. Billy Joel, You May be Right.

MISS RIGHT. I think you're right up his alley.

CHARLOTTE. It feels so right.

MISS RIGHT. I'm sure you're right. Do you write?

CHARLOTTE. Right now I'm working on a book called the "Right Way to Write."

MISS RIGHT. It is looking like the right combination.

CHARLOTTE. Is it all right if I write some things down?

MISS RIGHT. Certainly, it's your right.

(**CHARLOTTE** *takes out a notebook and pen. She begins to write with her left hand.*)

Oh, this is right out of left field.

CHARLOTTE. Excuse me?

MISS RIGHT. Just when you think the right one comes along.

CHARLOTTE. Is there a problem?

MISS RIGHT. You write with your left hand.

CHARLOTTE. Yes.

MISS RIGHT. That's not right.

CHARLOTTE. Oh dear.

MISS RIGHT. You're in the wrong place. Right around the corner is the Left Bank. They're the right place for you.

CHARLOTTE. The Left Bank?

MISS RIGHT. That's right. They take our leftovers.

CHARLOTTE. But things seemed so right here.

MISS RIGHT. They are right, but not for you.

CHARLOTTE. If I had left my pen in my purse.

MISS RIGHT. It wouldn't matter. You can't be right.

CHARLOTTE. So I'm left out in the cold?

MISS RIGHT. There's nothing left for you here.

CHARLOTTE. Thank you for your time.

MISS RIGHT. Righto.

CHARLOTTE. It's best if I left now.

MISS RIGHT. Goodbye.

CHARLOTTE. Goodbye.

(**CHARLOTTE** *leaves.* **DANNY** *enters.*)

DANNY. Hello. Are you Miss Right?

MISS RIGHT. I am. Welcome to The Right Place.

DANNY. Thank you.

MISS RIGHT. How can I help you?

DANNY. The right woman is out there for me. Can you help me find her?

MISS RIGHT. Oh yes. You were quite right to come here. What are you looking for in Miss Right?

DANNY. She must be forthright.

MISS RIGHT. Of course.

DANNY. Often right in her opinions, but not always right.

MISS RIGHT. Yields the right of way to you when necessary.

DANNY. That's right.

MISS RIGHT. Intelligent?

DANNY. Right brained.

MISS RIGHT. Sense of humor?

DANNY. Riotously funny.

MISS RIGHT. Playful?

DANNY. With the right dance moves.

MISS RIGHT. Punctual?

DANNY. Right on time.

MISS RIGHT. Right-wing?

DANNY. Right in the middle.

MISS RIGHT. Patriotic?

DANNY. Knows the Bill of Rights.

MISS RIGHT. Fair?

DANNY. Believes in civil rights.

MISS RIGHT. Right-handed?

DANNY. Absolutely.

MISS RIGHT. Excellent. Now, a few questions about you.

DANNY. All right.

MISS RIGHT. Favorite cartoon?

DANNY. Dudley Do Right.

MISS RIGHT. Favorite movie?

DANNY. The Right Stuff.

MISS RIGHT. Favorite animal?

DANNY. Right whales.

MISS RIGHT. Color?

DANNY. Bright right green.

MISS RIGHT. Excellent. You are right-handed?

DANNY. Yes.

MISS RIGHT. But not under-handed?

DANNY. That's right.

MISS RIGHT. I think we are right on our way to finding Miss Right.

DANNY. But you're Miss Right.

MISS RIGHT. Yes, well...

DANNY. You have beautiful eyes.

MISS RIGHT. Thank you. Now...

DANNY. And a nice smile.

MISS RIGHT. You're very sweet.

DANNY. What's your name?

MISS RIGHT. Miss Right.

DANNY. What's your first name?

MISS RIGHT. My first name?

DANNY. Yes.

MISS RIGHT. Mary. Mary Right.

DANNY. Sounds like the right name for a matchmaker, Mary Right. May I call you Mary?

MISS RIGHT. I'm not sure if it would be right.

DANNY. Do you always have to be right?

MISS RIGHT. Yes.

DANNY. Why?

MISS RIGHT. I'm not sure.

DANNY. Then it's okay to be wrong, Mary.

MISS RIGHT. Miss Right.

DANNY. Mary, what would happen if you were wrong?

MISS RIGHT. I don't know.

DANNY. Then let's find out. Have dinner with me tonight.

MISS RIGHT. I can't.

DANNY. Why not?

MISS RIGHT. Because you're a client.

DANNY. A client who's looking for Miss Right. You're Miss Right, aren't you?

MISS RIGHT. I am, but not like that.

DANNY. How do you know?

MISS RIGHT. That I'm not your Miss Right?

DANNY. Yes.

MISS RIGHT. I don't.

DANNY. Then have dinner with me tonight.

MISS RIGHT. Perhaps I should ask you some more questions.

DANNY. Let me ask you some.

MISS RIGHT. But Mr...

DANNY. Do you like walks in the park?

MISS RIGHT. In the park on Wright Ave.

DANNY. Hot chocolate in front of a warm fireplace?

MISS RIGHT. It's all right on a winter's night.

DANNY. Beautiful sunsets and rainbows?

MISS RIGHT. From a cabana right on the beach.

DANNY. Hawaii at Christmas time?

MISS RIGHT. With the right person.

DANNY. Mary...

MISS RIGHT. Miss Right.

DANNY. Mary, it's all right to let go.

MISS RIGHT. Perhaps you're right.

DANNY. You don't have to be right all the time. You can be wrong.

MISS RIGHT. I can't be wrong, I'm right.

DANNY. Marry me.

MISS RIGHT. What?

DANNY. Sometimes you have to be wrong in order to be right.

(**DANNY** *hands* **MISS RIGHT** *a card.*)

MISS RIGHT. Daniel Wrong. Troubleshooter. If it's wrong, I'll make it right.

DANNY. Marry me.

MISS RIGHT. But you're Wrong.

DANNY. It could be right.

MISS RIGHT. How about dinner instead?

DANNY. The Halfway House on Middle Street?

MISS RIGHT. All righ...I'd like that.

DANNY. Me too.

(*Lights down.*)

PROPS

Purse
Pen
Small purse-sized notebook
Business card
Legal pad and pen
Desktop accessories